NEW GROUND

By

Nancy Dillingham

Publisher: Ralph Roberts
Vice-President: Pat Roberts

Editors: Susan Parker, Barbara Blood, Gayle Graham

Cover and Interior Design: Susan Parker

Parts of this book appeared previously in *The Arts Journal, Bay Leaves, A Carolina Literary Companion, Half Tones to Jubilee, The Lyricist* and *Victoria Press.*

"Stay All Night (Stay A Little Longer)" by Bob Wills, Tommy Duncan, Peer International.

10 9 8 7 6 5 4 3 2 1

Library of Congress Cataloging-in-Publication Data

Dillingham, Nancy, 1944-
   New ground / by Nancy Dillingham
      p.   cm. --
   ISBN 1-56664-134-9 (alk. paper)
      1. Women--Literary collections   I. Title.
PS3554.I4185N49   1998
   818'.5409--dc21   98-8790
                                                           CIP

WorldComm®—a division of Creativity, Inc.—is a full-service publisher located at 65 Macedonia Road, Alexander NC 28701, distributed to the trade by Alexander Books. Phone (828) 252–9515, Fax (828) 255–8719. For orders only: 1-800-472-0438. Visa and MasterCard accepted.

This book is also available on the internet in the **Publishers CyberMall.** Set your browser to http://www.abooks.com and enjoy the many fine values available there.

CONTENTS

*To my mother
and in memory of my father*

Foreword

There is often a large element of chance in the way that one comes to read and admire a contemporary writer. I had come across the work of Nancy Dillingham almost accidentally in a few periodicals, skimmed it swiftly and then, in later hours, found that it had stayed in my mind for no reason I could put a name to.

The pieces I had found seemed to me a little unpolished and in a sense unfinished. They did not "conclude" in the ordinary way that stories are supposed to—and, in fact, they seemed less to be stories than vignettes. Actually, they seemed to belong to that old-fashioned genre, the "sketch," a term that earlier writers have used to signal that their compositions aimed not at lofty heights and grandiose ambitions, but strove instead to record accurately and feelingly small situations, minor episodes that gave insight into some recesses of the human spirit that writers of grander purpose did not care to investigate.

What made this author's work memorable, I decided, was her earnestness of purpose, her refusal to back off from a situation, to prettify or heighten tone with rhetorical device, and her acceptance—almost matter-of-fact—of the essential nature of her characters. There is something a little dim, even a little dun-colored, in Nancy Dillingham's presentations. It is as if she does not choose understatement as a literary method but sees life in such undistressed but fatalistic terms that illness, accident, disappointment, violence and death are no more than expectable occurrences. She expresses no outrage and hardly any disapproval toward the modes of conduct that result in disaster. Why should she? These were inherent in the makeup of her characters; they would be inevitably manifest, sooner or later, in one kind of strong action or another.

7

All this means that she has a *vision* and that in turn signifies, as I have discovered in reading *New Ground*, that the whole is much greater than the sum of its parts. Here is an odd but utterly genuine book, one that tastes of experience in its every line. The lines are not entirely graceful every time, but they are the more telling for their lack of finish. What is important is that *New Ground* exhibits vision, that quality to which technique is always secondary.

A writer with vision will exhibit certain constancies in her work. In these stories and poems we can see that the men may weep, yet will not talk; that there is violence frequently visited upon women but that it is thoughtless, hardly intentional; that men are often damaged physically, mentally, or morally and that the women take it upon themselves to care for them. The main theme in *New Ground* is the relationships between men and women, but where one might expect dialogue, or some give-and-take of thoughts and feelings, the incidents seem to happen in an abyss of silence. Here are pages in which muteness is so continual, so pervasive, so appalling it achieves a dimension of dread that physical violence usually does not attain.

Yet, for all her severity of outlook, Nancy Dillingham is not a dour or bitter or gloomy writer. Things are as they are in her world and this very condition of their being is what caused her to write of them. She could have fashioned them to a more contemporary taste; she could have falsified, though I have the impression this possibility never even occurred to her. Instead, she has chosen to follow her own light and report what her vision discovers. The easy way is not her way:

I'd rather float
with a discerning eye
earning my eternity

than to arrive
surprised
in paradise

Fred Chappell
Poet laureate of North Carolina
July 17, 1998

PROLOGUE

Providence

> "Women have no wilderness in them,
> They are provident instead,
> Content in the tight hot cell of their hearts . . ."
> —Louise Bogan

I

Her skin, like paper that has been folded many times and carried in someone's pocket like an ancient memory to be taken out and looked at again and again—dry, brittle, creased with fine wrinkles—is thin to the point of transparency, and, as she talks, a blue vein on her high forehead pulsates. When one of her hands (soft and tiny, with fingers like thin, pink sacs) suddenly flutters through the air to make a point and accidentally brushes against one of the reporter's, it is hot to the touch—her heart beating, it seems, in her hand.

Although the voice, rising as her fingers flutter, is surprisingly strong for someone her age, the earnest young man thinks how fragile she looks with her wisps of gray hair above that high forehead. He is reminded of the time many years ago when he stood on tiptoe cautiously peering at some small birds in their nest, their defenselessness overwhelming him—their eyes big and sightless, their mouths open, their bodies (featherless except for some soft, gray fuzz here and there) pink and pulsating. . . .

II

Her bare toes dig into the soft, sandlike dirt, little puffs of it rising and falling delicately before her as she walks up the lane. The big house stands at the end of the lane, a formidable awaiting.

11

She goes up the steps to the front door, lifts her arm, raises the heavy door knocker, and brings it down hard. The noise is so loud that she jumps back. The door is jerked open, and shiny boots (not creased and mud-caked like those of her father) rise toward a tall figure in a frock coat, his heavy, black brows flecked with gray. She looks up into the face. "My daddy sent me," she says in a clear, resolute voice. She is eleven years old.

III

She stands plaiting her younger sister's hair, feeling the smooth silkiness of the long, shiny, cream-colored strands slipping through her fingers as she laces them in and out.

Her father stands in front of the fireplace, his elbows resting on the mantel, his head bowed. Although she can't see his face, she knows that, if she could, it would hold a look she has seen many times before—one of desperation. His voice is low and too calm as he speaks. "I can't pay the big house," he says. Her mother, scraping potatoes in the kitchen, suddenly stops, and the girl imagines in the quiet that the swishing of the hair through her fingers makes the only discernible noise—except, perhaps, for her father's heart.

Later, as they sit down to fried potatoes and cornbread, her father speaks again in that voice, measured and controlled. "This land is all we've got. If we lose it, we'll be out in the big road. I was counting on the corn for payment this year. But this drought . . ." He shakes his head, and his voice trails off. Then her father suddenly looks at her. "The Man has offered to take you in place of the payment. He has promised to take care of you and to be good to you until you are sixteen." He takes a deep breath. "Then he wants to marry you." She feels faint and sick as she hears her father continue. "This family, of course, will make the decision together. Your mother and I couldn't bear the thought of losing you, but I think it would kill us all to lose this land after we've given the best years of our lives to it." His voice gives out suddenly, but he continues to look at her, the oldest child in the family.

She looks deep into her brother's and sister's eyes and speaks for the first time. "My brother, my sister, and I vote that I go to the big house, don't we?" Her brother and sister nod their heads slowly and obediently, uncomprehendingly. Her mother sucks in her breath, and her father puts his head in his hands. She rises from the table and stands between her mother and father, an arm resting on each of their shoulders.

IV

The man with the heavy, black brows with the flecks of gray in them takes her into the house and cares for her. The first day he leads her around the staircase into the dining room. He puts one arm carefully on her shoulder and speaks to the woman who is serving his lunch. "Get her some food and then see to it that she has clothes and shoes." The woman nods and takes her into the kitchen where she eats her meals for the next four years.

When she is fifteen, she is served her meals in the dining room with him. They eat at opposite ends of the table. At first, he eats as if only he were there. Then he begins to look at her and, finally, to talk to her, formally at first, offering only pleasantries. She observes that he looks at her directly only when he is silent, never when he talks. Instead, he looks at the clock mounted on the wall just above her head as if he were waiting for time to pass.

On the eve of her sixteenth birthday, she hears his footsteps stop at her door instead of going on down the hall to his room. She listens as he opens the door slowly and closes it gently behind him. She is not surprised, for she has been awaiting this moment for five years now. Wordlessly and deliberately, it seems, he sits down on the edge of the bed, takes off his boots, and drops them to the floor with a soft thud.

Some time later, just as deliberately, he puts his boots back on in the darkness and leaves. He has not spoken a word. She listens until she hears his door close and sees in her mind the practiced motions as he sits on his own bed and drops his boots to the floor. She hears the mattress sink with a little sigh as he slings his weight onto it. Only then does she put down the covers and open the curtains for the moon to come in. She lies until dawn on top of the covers, letting only the moon's rays touch her, their cool comfort cradling her. Over the years, the moon has become her best friend, bringing to her, in her fantasies, as it does tonight, members of her family with whom she talks until dawn.

The next day, on her sixteenth birthday, he marries her as he had promised her father.

V

Until the day he dies, he never sleeps all night in her bed. But one night (as he lies on the opposite side of the bed before he rises to put on his boots to leave), out of desperation—after years of silence and because she is drowning—she reaches out and hears her voice calling his name. It becomes an incantation as she whispers it over and over again. Only then does she know that she can survive.

Later, after he has gone to his room, she opens up the curtains and only the moon's clear light shines in. The shadowy forms of her family have now dissolved forever; she hears in her mind only the sound of her own voice calling his name over and over again.

VI

Still, there are many kinds of silence. During the following years, she has seven children, all of them stillborn except the last. Each time, she is deathly sick. Each time she feels the life flow prematurely from her body, helpless to do anything to hold it back.

The last one, the one that lives for a short time, has no eyelashes or fingernails. She feeds it with a medicine dropper and warms it with a big rock, heated and wrapped in a blanket. She holds it in her arms and watches it die, covering its face with a cloth dipped in camphor, rocking it until the doctor comes. For years afterward, she can't bear the smell of camphor.

VII

That fateful day burns in her mind like a struck match. She is doing the wash in a big, black pot hung over a smoldering fire. She has just picked up the wooden stick leaning to one side of the pot to poke and stir the boiling clothes, the steam wetting her face, when she sees him coming up the lane. Immediately she knows something is wrong because he never comes out of the fields until lunchtime; he comes in through the kitchen, washes up at the sink, wets and combs his hair in the little glass hanging by the window, goes into the dining room, takes out his pocket watch, winds it, and checks its time against the big clock on the wall over the table then sits down to eat. But today he is here in the morning, and something is wrong.

14

She drops the stick, wiping her face with her apron, walking toward him, quickening her pace until she is running. He, too, is walking faster now, though his gait is uncharacteristically unsteady. Coming closer now, she sees that his face is red and that he is gasping for breath. He reaches out one arm jerkily towards her and tries to speak. In the instant before his body hits hers, she notices that his face is contorted and that one side is curiously slack. He falls heavily on her. The impact jolts, threatening to knock her down, the body still lean and muscular.

Out of breath and struggling, she gets him the rest of the way up the lane and into the house. From that day on, he never again speaks a word or takes a step.

VIII

She stands under one large tree, dwarfed by its height, her hair pulled up high on her head, her hands clasping the back of a shiny, arched, wooden chair on wheels. He sits in the chair, immobile. The photographer, catching the best light of the day, covers his head with the black cloth, peers at them through his box, and, squeezing the ball in his hand, snaps the photograph with a small explosion. She is thirty-six years old; he is sixty.

IX

She speaks his name softly, from habit now, as she wheels him out onto the side porch. The morning air is fresh. She positions him beside the railing where she has set his breakfast bowl. She holds his face with one hand and feeds him with the other. His face is as closed now as it was fifty years ago when she first came up the lane, and she has perhaps just as many questions now as she had then. But it is a familiar lane and face now, and she knows the planes of each. His silence is a steady companion now. With a practiced hand, whispering his name over and over again, she cajoles him into eating. The wind carries his name down the lane, blowing it away with the little puffs of dirt.

Some time later, before the clock's practiced hands point straight up, the wind takes his breath away, carries it, too, down the lane, and scatters it over the land.

X

The voice is whispery now, like a quiet wind through the room. The house smells of ripe apples and old newspaper. It is late now, and the shadows of the trees play with the curtains. She fingers the photograph. The sleek, empty glasses stand on the tray in little puddles, having long since shed their frosty wetness. The visit has come to an end. She rises and walks the young reporter out. Through the screen door she calls a farewell, her voice once again clear and strong. As he turns, he sees her silhouetted against the light from the big windows at the other end of the house, the hall long and narrow before her.

NEW GROUND

Moving Pictures

Outside, the dampness of the summer night drapes itself around them like a light sweater. The youngest is asleep in the father's arms as they all pile into the old car. The roughness of the seats against their shorts-clad legs nudges them like a cat's tongue. The night is so clear it is perfect; the moon, a distant dime's worth of cool light dropped on the smooth, dark cloth of the sky.

As the small car moves through the quiet countryside in the night air, around the curving road toward home, its dim headlights hugging the next curve, all of the children (except the youngest, who sleeps by their father on the front seat) sit on the back seat together, their bare feet stretched out in front of them on the floorboard, their fingers curled around the edges of the seat for a good grip, their heads thrown back, watching the moon out the back window. First, it follows the car, bouncing just above their heads; then it suddenly appears over to the right, hiding behind a bump in the mountain; and, finally, it is in front of them, leading them.

This game of watching the moon keeps them awake until they rattle over the loose planks of the bridge, move over the blackberry-lined dirt road, and grind up the rocky bank home where they tumble out sleepily to bed. . . .

Each Saturday night after supper, during the summer, they all pile into the car—except their mama, of course, who uses the time to wash or iron or clean—and drive down to the local grocery store where they watch television in Mae Ivy's living room, built on to the back of the store. Mrs. Ivy, the owner of the store, walks in and out between intervals of waiting on customers, sucking cola from a bottle. As she holds the bottle up in her white, sleeveless arm, the children think some of the cola must run directly into it, it looks so fat.

Saturday night is a busy time at the store, clusters of cars coming and going, loud voices and laughter punctuating the flickering, blue images on the small television screen, injecting themselves into Perry Como's solo as he perches casually on a stool, or into Matt Dillon's stiff-legged shoot-out.

The country store is this family's Saturday night at the picture show. Barefoot, the children troop in behind their father, through the narrow walking space between the whirring freezers and shelves lined with crackers and cookies, past the bread tray, to the counters of candy, chewing tobacco, and cigarettes near the cash register, past the crowd, into the narrow door leading to the darkened living room, feeling the coolness of the concrete floor seeping into their feet and the hot, blowing air from the freezers on their bare legs, smelling the unique smell of the store, produced by the mingling of candy and tobacco and the newness of paper bags and cellophane wrapping.

The children fidget a little at first, settling in. They aren't crazy about Perry Como's musical interlude, but they sometimes recognize one of the songs because they have heard it at home when they put their ears to the small radio, pressing their hands against its warm back to keep the sound from fading out. (The radio is encased in plastic with a big crack down the middle of it where one of the children accidentally got tangled in its cord and pulled it off the high chest of drawers and broke it. They bandaged it with some black, sticky tape they found in their daddy's old tool box so that it looks now like a cracked skull, a head talking and talking out of control as they switch its dial back and forth.)

They settle down in earnest, however, for the western features. Sometimes the harsh tales of "Gunsmoke" leave them trembling or cause them to suck a piece of ice down their throats from the cola that Daddy buys from the machine out front. But they know the tales are not real when Daddy reaches forward and pats them on their backs, laughing softly. As they sit lined up on the couch in the darkened living room, the drama of life,

20

on-screen and off, dips in and around them (like the moon), as far removed from them as the moon they watch from the back seat of the car as it carries them safely home.

One Saturday night, when the gunshots on the screen are echoed by those outside and when suddenly there are no intervals of laughter interrupting the drama on the flickering screen, Mrs. Ivy comes through the narrow door and speaks to their father who is sitting at the end of the couch in a straight-backed chair with the sleeping baby in his arms. You better get the children out of here, she says.

The children lean forward on the couch in one motion, sucking in their breaths collectively, their little mouths forming small O's. Then they all scramble up quickly and follow their daddy out through Mae Ivy's side door, making their way to the car parked out of the way of traffic.

As they walk, they can see a circle of overall-clad men gathered around a pickup truck under the pools of icy-blue light from the big, round lamps that hang over the gas pumps. The men's heads jerk toward the sound, and, at the sight of four small children trailing their daddy (who carries another in his arms), their stiff, little shadows jumping up and down like soldiers behind them, the men hover closer to the truck, closing the circle, protecting it—and the children. But it is too late. The little troopers have already seen the body beside the truck.

They are just getting in the car, the father hurriedly sticking the sleeping child through the door onto the seat beside him, when the small, white ambulance arrives, followed closely by a brown sheriff's car with a gold star on its side and a flashing light on top. The light flashes across the back window of the ancient car where the children now gather, protected by its rusty shell.

But it has touched them, and that night, as they lie sleeping in their beds, it touches them again, in their dreams, sending their arms flailing, causing them to whimper softly, as the moon hovers distantly overhead.

New Ground

When he was drunk—so drunk he couldn't feed himself—she would stand in the kitchen (stifling hot, summer and winter, from the wood stove), methodically, almost mechanically, wiping the sweat with his red bandanna handkerchief as it popped out on his early-balding head and trickled in narrow, crooked creeks down his face, which was tanned leather except above his eyebrows where his cap kept it unnaturally white and vulnerable-looking, like a woman's body.

He was a big, hulking, simple man—a child with a fourth-grade education. He married, at seventeen, a woman fifteen years his senior. His wife was a widow with three children, and she guided him for thirty-five years with a strong hand.

He was a farmer, and, when he received his annual tobacco check, it was always in her name (it was her land). When he took his calves to the stockyard, it was always with her along, in a man's cap, carefully watching the bargaining.

When he could get away in the green '49 pickup without her seated on the other side, one fat arm resting on the rolled-down window, he was deliberately reckless. He couldn't hold his liquor very well. Always a rather stiff, awkward man, he was, when drunk, forever falling into things and, in turn, cursing himself in a rather forgetful way.

Once when he came to visit, it was blowing blue snow and was so cold that the drinking water froze in the bucket on the sink. His boots were only partly laced, and he was shivering in his overalls and the greasy hunting jacket he always wore—this time, over only long-handles. He sat in the chair that made him look cramped up and tried to roll a cigarette. He took out his Prince Albert and two or three papers—he tried blowing them apart and couldn't. Spilling out tobacco, he licked the sides together and tried to strike a match on a galluse fastener to light one of the clamped, spit-dampened ends. It kept going out, and he kept striking matches and losing tobacco out the side, muttering continuously. He nodded sleepily once or twice and kept asking "Ain't that right, Son?", shaking his head and laughing over the time he and my father and some other men had gone 'coon hunting and lost their dogs and the way back to camp to boot. As usual, he called us from where we were (peeking around the corner to the living room) and gave us money, dropping change down the sides of the chair without noticing it. (Once, in front of him, his wife told how he gave her own three children a lot of money just after the tobacco was sold one year and how he asked for it back when he sobered up. He laughed and shook his head. "I'm a sonavabitch," he said.) That night, like all the others, he could be persuaded to go home only when we promised to "come up" sometime. My father drove him home in the old '49 truck and walked back in the snow.

His wife always told him, however matter-of-factly, that if she ever caught him with another woman she would kill him—and the woman. He believed her; yet he often went down the road and found one of those blank-faced, inevitably pretty girls who sat with their mothers and sisters on their porches and followed (with their eyes) the cars beyond the falling clotheslines and the grassless yards filled with junked cars.

Everyone says that's where he went that balmy, spring evening. (My brother was one of the ones who found him, and he told my brother, like a child caught doing something wrong, that he was sorry and that he didn't know why he did it.) They found him sitting in a sheltered meadow in the mountains on a stump, holding his head bowed between his legs. The truck had turned over on its side and apparently spilled its contents through one now-open door. The young girl in her white blouse and red, full skirt lay on a smooth, mound-like area with her head propped upon a rock. She could have been sleeping, but she was not. They asked him what had happened. He looked up mutely, crying quietly, his big shoulders heaving. They righted the truck and took her away. That's when he told my brother. He had wanted to drive up in the mountains to the waterfall. They had rounded a curve, hit a fallen rock, careened off the road, and flipped. It had happened so quickly. She was sitting close to him on the seat, holding his "chaser"—his 7-Up—as usual. The next thing he knew, they were falling out of one side of the truck onto the ground, he on top of her. (I could imagine even then his head on her warm breast, her soft skin beneath his rough beard.) He called her name and knew. He pushed up off her, smoothed her hair and clothes, picked her up, clear of the wreck, and placed her on the smooth, cool ground.

My brother had wanted to comfort him, but could only take him home. (The authorities said it was an accident, pure and simple.)

Next morning, the sun was shining very brightly. I can still see him from the distance of the back seat of our old, faded car as he gently led his mule to the edge of the field, hitched up the plow, and began to break new ground.

He died yesterday (one month after his wife), a long time having passed since that evening and morning, many fields having been plowed and harvested. But I remember most the sight of the man, suddenly old, as he cracked the reins, clucked to the mule, and doggedly began to push the plow into the dark, mysterious earth.

Life Signs

The night before my sister was born, the little store across the road burned to the ground. Grandma told my mother not to look at the fire because it might mark the child. Mother, lying in the hot July night, looked as big in bed as the billowing sheets that she had hung on the clothesline earlier that day. Her dark hair, limp and moist, clung to the sides of her whitened face. I lay at the foot of the bed thinking that now Grandpa could no longer walk to the store for graham crackers—he called them "greyhounds"—and knock on the front gate with his cane that had the dog's head carved on top of it and tell me to come and get them and pat me on the head before walking up the lane to his house.

What's wrong? Honey. Are you sick? Mother asked anxiously. Come here and let me feel your head and see if it's hot. Wordlessly I obeyed. She pressed her warm palm on my forehead and smiled at me, her attention not wholly on me. I could see that she was worried, and I felt her fear. Maybe the store's catching on fire *was* a bad omen as Grandma had said.

The next morning, Mother, uncharacteristically, was still in bed. Her face looked swollen. The day was muggy, even before breakfast. Grandma was still there fussing about. Usually at a birthing (I learned later) the midwife down the road came (along with women of the community) to help out. Grandma had sent for her last night, but she was not here today. I later learned, also, that Mother had asked Grandma not to bring anyone in. I don't want everyone hovering around me, especially women, my mother had told her. That's why Grandma was so nervous—all the responsibility was on her. He'll kill me if something happens, she said, meaning my father.

All morning I hung at the foot of the bed as I had done the night before. About lunch time, one of my grown cousins came down from Grandma's house and took my older sister and me up the lane. Let's have a play party, she said, smiling one of those grown-up smiles. I allowed her to take my hand, but only reluctantly.

At Grandma's we played "house" and pretended, with acorns, to drink coffee from cups and saucers, but my mind was elsewhere: a nagging heaviness hung there in the background, gnawing.

Later that afternoon, our cousin led us back down the lane. When we went into the house, Mother was still in bed, but a long, scrawny, red, crying baby lay beside her. It looked funny and strange, but everybody was smiling so I thought everything must be all right. Mother motioned us closer, and we looked at the baby but were afraid to touch it.

That event happened in July, and, in the fall of that same year, another event occurred: my grandfather died. (The "brindle cat," his favorite name for my older sister, and I had sat on his lap that summer while my mother had gone to pick blackberries in the pasture above his house.) Daddy came in and said: Poppy died. No one else had "died" in the family (that I could remember) and I could remember no one else having given birth before my mother; one event seemed just as mysterious as the other.

Before the funeral, they brought my grandfather back to Grandma's house to lie in state. On the morning of the funeral, Daddy got ready and wanted to take us with him to see Grandpa. The children aren't old enough to understand, my mother said. My father said in that voice: I want them to see Poppy for one last time. Mother just looked at him and watched from the door as we walked out of sight up the lane.

When we arrived, the house was filled with strangers—more people than I had ever seen. They were lined up against the wall talking in hushed voices, which they lowered even further when we passed by. My sister and I sat down in the floor in a corner. My father disappeared for a while, and, when he came back to get us, he led us into the cool sitting room with the pale green velvet divan, used only for company. All of the family were there, hovering at the foot of the casket, very pale and very silent, and, looking at them, I saw the same fear in their faces as I had felt the night my sister was born, and I felt the same anxiety as I had felt then—at something new, mysterious, unfathomable, tangibly elusive.

Into the silence my father spoke, saying he wanted us to see Grandpa. He lifted both of us up and held us over the casket. The padded lid was raised and turned back to one side. Grandpa was still and white, dressed in a black suit and tie and a white shirt with a stiff-looking collar. I hardly recognized him. I was accustomed to seeing him in his old, faded pants held up with his green and red suspenders over his long-handled underwear, sometimes with his teeth out, his hair standing up on his head in a little tuft. My father's sister, my aunt, had raised the casket lid and, after straightening the white carnation pinned to his suit, was combing the soft, sparse, almost-white, baby-fine hair neatly over to one side. It reminded me of the way my mother combed the baby's hair, while it was still damp, just after she had given it a bath, over her finger, in a big curl on top.

As my father held us there, my grandmother, in black, suddenly came out of her bedroom. Her hair, usually combed back neatly and secured with gray combs, was disheveled and down, her eyes unfocusing. One of my aunts quickly led her out of the room back into the bedroom. Had she really been there or had I seen an apparition? I was accustomed to seeing Grandma, blue eyes twinkling, in the kitchen in an apron spooning hot grease from the little silver measuring cup that she kept in the warming closet of the stove onto the top of the big, fat biscuits before putting them in the Warm Morning to rise up and brown to a flaky crispness. Today her eyes had looked dull, unrecognizing.

Suddenly, everyone and everything appeared transformed. Even my father, the man who now held me up in one arm, looked strange in his gray overcoat and white silk scarf, the one that my mother had given him with his initial on it, the one that was usually folded in a flat, white box between tissue paper and stored in the cedar chest in the bedroom. It occurred to me, much later, that the look on his face (one of astonishment) as he viewed his own father, a stranger now in a stiff, black suit, was perhaps the same as the one on my own face when I first looked at my mother that hot, muggy night, as the fire burned its omen into my heart: I, too, had viewed a stranger, someone unfamiliar—in a new dimension then—pale, wan, and expiring, giving new life.

Rust

The clouds were black, tinged with intense purple. They seemed to boil. It's hailed somewhere, she would say.

I walked up the curving lane to her house in the dampened, sun-spotted air, now saturated with the sweet, clinging smell of lilac. I crossed the footlog and walked between the two bunching bushes filled with blossoms spoiled like fruit with patches of iron rust.

It was early morning, and she liked to drink her coffee on the front porch. I found her there pinching off dead leaves from the sultanas that she had moved out in the sun for a little while in their wooden flower boxes. (She would give me cuttings when they grew in their water-like substance.)

I had come to comfort her—not to talk but to sit quietly in the chairs bottomed with strips of tire tubing. We usually didn't talk much, so my sitting would be sufficient.

He had died with a heart attack, very sudden and very early one morning. She had brought coffee to his bed just as she had done for forty or fifty years before. He had clutched at his chest, and that was it.

But this morning she talked more than usual—not about that but of an earlier time. She set her cup in its saucer after slowly pouring the steaming, clay-colored liquid back and forth, blowing on it to cool it, then, finally, carefully, sipping mouthfuls from the saucer. She sighed, resting her hands on the whitened places on the rocker's arms, closed her eyes, and leaned silently backward. She began, dreamlike, to talk.

It was during the Hoover panic. He had been logging on the pinnacle that day, and she was cooking at the logging camp. It was almost dark when they reached the main road leading out of the boundary toward home. It had begun to rain—a real gully-washer, he called it. When they reached the bridge, the creek was up, and they knew the planks were black and swollen.

She raised a hand with fingers spread and signaled toward the main road and the bridge leading to the dirt road, crooking upward now as it had then.

The horse stumbled on a raised plank, and the unexpectedly hard jolt threw her from behind him and into the creek. She was already drenched, but the rushing waters slapped hard against her. She gasped for breath and some time later caught on the brace under the bridge. She shook from head to toe as she pulled up on the far side of the bank. Like lightning slowed down, the moon came from behind the blowing clouds. The only noise now was the roaring of the mountains and the sluicy water. She heard the old horse pawing against the rocks and saw it just beyond the bridge. She ran toward the empty saddle and held on. Some time later, she looked back toward the bridge and saw him lying there. Her legs like water, she walked to him and knelt. She felt his face surprisingly wet against the drying wind and realized that he was not hurt but that he was silently crying. She helped him up. He said nothing, but they stood close together on the bridge and watched the white patches of waves disappear in the rolling water. Much later, they heard a rooster crow and realized that the roaring mountain had quieted and that it was still—the stillest part of the day. They walked home in the graying dawn leading the horse.

She went suddenly silent, and I saw that her eyes were following the clouds. She began to rock, and I counted the creaking sounds in regular patterns of four until they stopped.

He never mentioned anything about that as long as he lived, she said very quietly—to herself, I think, more than to me.

I saw her hand jerk toward her face. I looked out to the garden where volunteer potato vines would soon be appearing among the larkspur and poppy.

She rose from her chair and emptied the grounds from her cup into the flower boxes. (She often said they helped the plants to grow.) She took hold of my arm, and we walked, as usual, around the side porch to the back door. We stepped down on the smooth rock step and walked to one of the lilac bushes where she found for me an almost rust-free cluster.

Grandma's Baby Boy

He was Grandma's youngest child—her baby boy—and my father's brother. He bit his fingernails and walked in a sidling manner. He knew his way around the kitchen as well as Grandma. A light sleeper, he made the coffee in the morning and cooked breakfast, complete with gravy and biscuits. A choosy eater, he loved sweets. His specialty was apple pie. Whistling, an apron tied neatly around his waist, he worked patiently around the old Warm Morning stove, crossing sticks of kindling and stove wood neatly in the crackling box.

One day, while playing on the porch, we must have interrupted his cooking with too much noise. He walked around the side of the house with a circle of dough on his face, the eyes, nose, and mouth cut out. It's a haint, Grandma said in a stage whisper. Scared to death, we began to run home down the lane, looking back, too late, seeing Grandma doubled over with laughter.

He was always as neat and clean as a pin. His hair, parted so straight and combed back on each side, was shiny and so black that it looked blue. We asked Mother if he dyed it. She said she didn't think so—he was too young to black his hair. One thing about it, he could always get a woman, my grandma used to say, punching the nearest adult in the ribs with her sharp elbow, her small, blue eyes jumping like marbles. He could charm the bark off a tree. Of course, she reckoned, his two brief marriages had just been sad mistakes.

He had first married a divorcée five years his senior who had her own apartment in town and a car to boot. (My uncle didn't own a car since he never really had a job.) The marriage had ended unceremoniously and suddenly after an unfortunate misunderstanding during which (according to gossip) he had pulled his wife across the room by her long hair. The next day, she had decided, simultaneously, to have her hair cut short in a new permanent and to get a divorce.

His next marriage was to a waitress in a truck stop. He said she was so pretty that she could have been a doll if only she'd had the breath slapped out of her. I saw her once, and she *did* look something like a doll with her piled-up hair dyed so blonde it looked flaxen, her eyelashes curled and mascaraed in a stiff, backward "c," and her lips painted the brightest pink. (Daddy said they would glow in the dark.) He bought a set of rings and gave them to her on their second date, hocking his class ring which Daddy had bought. (He had lacked two weeks graduating from high school, quitting to join the navy, getting homesick and going AWOL and finally being dishonorably discharged.) Unfortunately, her husband, a trucker, came back unexpectedly that same week from California.

He met Oley (Grandma called her "Oleo Margarine") when he was in the hospital. (The trucker's punches packed quite a wallop.) She was a nurse's aide and took him under her wing, bringing him cigarettes and silver tips, which he loved. She even gave him a little gold lighter which had once belonged to her son. She was very short and chubby with white legs fat like lard on which she wore little white anklet socks folded over once. Her short, fat feet were stuffed into sensible, black oxfords which she worked in. She was usually dressed in a navy uniform which she also wore to work. She must have been fifteen or twenty years older than my uncle. (Daddy said she was ugly as homemade sin. Mother frowned at him and shook her head and said she was just plain.)

Although he often stayed in town with her, they came out on Saturday nights with one of my aunts and her husband who also lived in town. My aunt worked with Oley. The evenings were predictable. They gathered around the table in the kitchen to play cards. Oley sat on my uncle's lap and giggled. We children just stared until Mother took us into the living room and tuned in the Grand Ole Opry on the static-filled radio, giving us a leg of saltine crackers to eat on. The smoke would get thicker and bluer and someone would bring out the jar of white lightning. (Mother didn't drink, but Grandma often told her in conversation: "Just pour it down the front of your dress like I used to do, Honey, and they'll think you do and leave you alone!") The laughter would get louder and continue until three or four in the morning, long after Mother had come and taken us to bed. (She always came in at midnight and told us it was time to go to bed since we had to get up the next morning and go to Sunday School.) Sometimes my uncle would pass out—he couldn't drink very much without feeling the effects—and they would move him to the couch where Oley hovered solicitously with black coffee.

One Saturday night, they all came early. It was a muggy summer night with rumbling thunder threatening a storm. The men (instead of playing cards, as usual) had decided to go frog gigging in a neighbor's pond. My uncle decided on the way home with the frog legs that he wanted some of "Mommie's fried chicken" and stole one of another neighbor's old sitting hens. By the time they got back to our house, it was raining like it was coming out of buckets, but my uncle insisted on going on up to my grandma's house. Everybody put on old coats and hats and scarves, and we piled into Daddy's '49 Ford. Packed like sardines, the windshield wipers doing no good—the rain was coming down in sheets over the windows— the windows fogging up from our breath, we spun and slid but sluggishly climbed the steeply winding lane to my grandma's house. While the car protested against my father's attempts to back it up and head it downhill before we got out, Grandma appeared at the back door, her lantern bobbing, shading her bespectacled eyes against the torrent of rain and darkness, trying to figure out who was crazy enough to come out in such weather. As we hurried across the footlog up to the rock steps of the side porch leading to the back door, she held the light up for us. Seeing us standing in our big coats, soaking wet, water running off them to our feet, she exclaimed, Why you little birdies! What do they mean, bringing you all out in this rain? She led us in.

Grandma's house was not wired for electricity, so we waited for her to go in front of us with the kerosene lamp which she picked up off the cabinet in the kitchen as she set the lantern down. She led us through the dining room into the room where she stayed. Another lamp sat on the table beside her bed with little strips of red paper in the base, floating in the kerosene. We took off our coats and hung them on the two straight-backed chairs she kept by the stove, turning them, back first, toward it. We took off our wet shoes and set them under the stove, turning round and round in front of it. Fan your dress tails and get them dry, she said. The grown-ups had come in by now, blown out the lantern, taken off their coats, and gone back into the kitchen. Grandma with them, they took one lamp and left the other one for us.

Grandma's bed was in her living room, and we sat on the edge of it. The flickering lamp made big, black, moving shadows on the wall, and we sat in the room listening to the rain beating on the tin roof, sounding like hail, and to the crackling fire that Grandma had stoked up (even in the summertime, especially on a damp night, Grandma had a fire) by lifting the door with a gloved hand and taking two or three lumps of coal from the coal bucket and tossing them in. Grandma was an avid reader and read anything anyone discarded. We saw the familiar stacks of the *Christian Science Monitor* and the *Grit* on the oilcloth-lined table that sat beside her bed under the stern ovals of her mother and father and the big grandfather clock that struck hourly with soft, orchestrated booms. (Grandma was a great one for utilizing everything, and when she finished reading the papers she used them to line the tiny pantry off the dining room. When she opened it to give us a jar of her vanilla-flavored pickled beets or a snuff jar of blackberry jam, the smell of dried newspaper was sharp and acrid— like a jar of vinegar being opened.)

They cooked and cooked the chicken on the Warm Morning stove— Mother said it was the toughest chicken she had ever seen. The frog legs jumped so much as they were frying that Mother said they had to keep the lid pressed on them to keep them from jumping out of the pan onto the floor. (She claims to this day that some of the frog legs ended up under the stove.) It was hard to see how to cook by one lamp, and everyone was bumping into one another, the men leaned up against Grandma's cabinet, a bottle of whiskey nearby, carrying on while the women tried to cook.

Soon they piled everything on the dining room table, coming for us and taking the other lamp for one end of the long, wooden table.

When we were ready to leave, half-asleep, Grandma bundled us up again in our coats, by now, dry, crisp, and warm, and we put on our shoes, dried and stiff. The rain was still coming down, and, on the way to the car, ahead of us (Grandma was waiting for the grown-ups to get in before she let us run for it—You'll catch your deaths, she fussed), our uncle slipped on the footlog and fell into the branch. We heard him protesting, thinking him annoyed at getting his shoes wet and squishy and his clothes mussed. We heard everyone else clamoring over him, hearing Oley say, Can you get up,

36

Sugar? Grandma, waiting on the porch with us, lantern in hand, coatless, now ran forward in the rain, and we ran after her. Everyone fell back as she raised the smoldering globe over his face. The rain glistened on his blue-black hair, somehow still in place. His face was white and immobile, lying to one side at a strange angle. Oley now reached down and turned it upward. His neck's broken! she screamed.

Grandma took to her bed for a week or so—the doctors thought she had pneumonia and gave her up to die. She had a high fever and talked out of her head. But soon she was up and walking about, puttering in her flowers —turning her monkey faces to the sun, hoeing her see-roses with a fork, collecting some black, round seeds of the pretty-by-nights in an empty snuff tin. She began to talk about her baby boy again, laughing suddenly, recalling one of his escapades. Finally, Grandma said she believed it was all right after all: he was not really drunk (she remembered the tent preachers' admonitions that a drunk man cannot enter the kingdom of heaven)—he had only had a drink or two—and he had died happy, having just eaten his fill of his favorite meal.

Auntie

The summer that Daddy moved them in everybody said that he shouldn't allow Auntie (she was no one's aunt, yet everyone called her that) and her son to live in the bottom in the little house. (Daddy let them live there, rent free, in return for the son's help on the farm.) Furthermore, they said, Mother shouldn't let us children be around them because it was rumored that the son had had TB since he now began every sentence by clearing his throat. Uh-hem, he would begin, and then he would finish what he was saying.

Auntie was said to be a witch, and most of the children were afraid of her. She *did* look like one with the myriad of wrinkles on her aged face and a huge brown, soft-looking mole on the side of her somewhat hooked nose with its flat, flaring nostrils. But we were only slightly afraid of her, and when she walked, or rather hobbled, by our house in her shapeless dress of an indeterminate gray color, which reached down to her swollen, misshapen ankles and which was covered with three or four faded-out aprons, we followed at a distance, companionably silent.

The only person Auntie visited was my aunt, who would talk to anyone, she was so lonesome. She and Auntie would sit under the large shade tree by the side of the house and dip snuff. (Auntie taught us how to make a brush—she used hers for dipping; we used ours for brushing our teeth or for "dipping" cocoa and sugar from a lid. First, you cut off a piece of birch, take a sharp knife and cut up through the peeled part like you would an onion you were going to dice. Finally, you chew this end until it is soft.)

39

Snuff came in glasses that were later re-used for putting up jelly or drinking milk. Most of the womenfolk who dipped took out small amounts and carried it, for convenience, in little tins in their bosoms or aprons. Auntie and my aunt would take out these containers, tap on the top all the way around to dislodge the powder from the lid so as not to spill it when they opened it up. After opening the tin carefully, they took the birch brush, softened it with spittle, and swabbed it in the snuff. When the brush was thinly coated, they placed it into the sides of their mouths—in Auntie's case, between the gap in the front of her mouth where several teeth were missing. (Sometimes, if they didn't have a birch brush, they would use a little spoon for dipping, heaping it up, then placing its contents in the lower lip so that the lip protruded like it was swollen, their bottom teeth filling with the amber juice.) Then they would put the lid back on, snap the tin shut, and slip it back into their bosoms or their aprons, sit back in their rockers, cross their legs, and talk and spit and dip.

Auntie could cross her legs and still place both feet on the ground, a feat we had never seen accomplished before. When she crossed her legs, we could sometimes see her cotton stockings knotted just below the knee. Both she and my aunt were superstitious, and they often enthralled us with stories of people dying after a rooster crowed at sunset or about someone being chased off the mountain by a racer black snake that suspended itself in the air like waves or about someone's cow giving bloody milk after they stepped on a granddaddy.

As I said, we were a little bit afraid of Auntie, yet curiously drawn to her somehow. She taught us a chant that could make doodlebugs come out of their dirt mounds:

"Doodlebug, doodlebug,
come up, come up;
your house is on fire,
and your children all burning up."

Twice that summer we went through the bottom to the small shack where she lived. Once we sat on the stoop with her in the sun, listening to her talk in her rather coarse, flat voice. We never talked. Once she took us inside, although we had been forbidden to go any further than the door when we went with messages for the son about work that needed to be done—kindling split or tobacco plants pulled. Since it was summer, the fire was out in the fireplace, but a black pot sat to the side on the hearth still steaming and smelling of soup beans. There were only two rooms in the shack—a small kitchen and a living room crammed with two small, iron beds and boxes stacked everywhere. From under one of the beds, she pulled an ancient, black trunk with tarnished hinges. She opened it up, and it was filled with mementos—a black, cut glass necklace; a pink satin sachet pillow with an empty, fancy perfume bottle; the wooden leg of her other son who had lost a leg in the Second World War; letters and postcards. He went to all them "furrin" countries, she said as she held up a scalloped postcard with a picture of a huge tower. I felt like I had been transported to an exotic place. It was the same sensation I later experienced when I saw the film version of *Treasure Island* in the little dusty green audio-visual room at grammar school. I can still see the opening scene where the little boy comes up a windy, winding trail to the tavern, lifts the knocker and bangs on the door. From that moment on, a strange, mysterious world opens up. I can still see the sinister way the pirate sliced up an apple and feel the rocking of the ship and the creaking of the wood as they stepped aboard and hear the coarse croaking of the parrot with the shiny, green feathers as it perched on the pirate's shoulder.

That was the last time I saw Auntie. I heard Daddy and Mother talking conspiratorially in the kitchen one day. The next night we awoke to a huge fire burning in the bottom. The shack was ablaze. For a moment, before I was fully awake, the fiery light through the bedroom window startled and frightened me so much that I thought it was the "end of time" that I had heard so much about from the pulpit of our church during Sunday preaching and revivals or tent meetings. *Fire and brimstone shall destroy the earth* reverberated through my head, and I shook all over as I stood, a few minutes later, with my parents and sisters in front of our picture window and watched the fire shoot upward in great orange balls. I was horrified thinking that Auntie and her son had indeed been taken up in a great cloud of fire. Daddy didn't seem particularly worried and tried to reassure me. I was puzzled, for I had seen the horseplay and wisecracking and easy camaraderie between my father and the son.

The next day I was all prepared to see the bones or skeletons of Auntie and her son in the smoldering rubble. We poked gingerly in the remains of the shack with tobacco sticks, but all we could find was a piece of melted glass. I wondered if this was Auntie's empty perfume bottle. I imagined the flames licking the letters and postcards, and I mourned Auntie's loss.

41

After we questioned her and bothered her so much for answers, Mother finally told my sisters and me later that people in the community had threatened to burn the shack and its contents because they constituted a health hazard if Daddy didn't move Auntie and her son away. When he could take it no longer, Daddy had finally given in. He had secretly and quietly moved Auntie and her son in the middle of the night the day before he, himself, had set the shack on fire.

For several months after that, gossip and rumors were rampant. Whenever they could, people would corner my sisters and me—in the churchyard, at the store, at the little post office down the road—and try to question us about Auntie. We told them that on the night of the fire we had watched her and her son ascend into heaven in a cloud of fire. They looked askance at us and went away, mumbling or shaking their heads. Soon word was out that Auntie had cast a spell on us, that we were now "tetched," wild children that other children should stay away from. But all the children loved our stories, and we often laughed under the covers at night as we compared the tall tales we had concocted that day.

We didn't ask where Daddy had taken Auntie, but some time later as we were looking at the suckers and fireballs and jawbreakers in the glass containers lined up on the cabinet of the store, one of our neighbors came in looking like he had seen a ghost. He was white and shaken, and his voice was hoarse and queer as he told the storekeeper that he had just seen Auntie or her spirit walking on the road on the way to town. She looked hardly changed at all, he said, except that she had a red rag tied on her head, probably to cover the baldness where the fire had singed off her hair. We came up behind him then, thrusting our pennies out to the storekeeper. He took them hurriedly and put our choices in a little brown paper bag. They both stared at us like we were prophets like Jeremiah or Obadiah or something. We walked solemnly out of the store, very dignified, the screen door that read in orange letters "Colonial is Good Bread" banging behind us. Not until we were out of sight up the road did we double up with laughter.

For the rest of the summer, we had a field day with that story, embellishing it at every opportunity, creating imaginary meetings between Auntie and other members of the community. We were particularly graphic when recounting her vision of the Gates of Hell.

A Convenient Season

I sat in the swing on the big, front porch scuffing my toes on the planks and watching the preacher coming around the red, clay bank to the grassy yard, carrying his Bible underhanded and whistling. Our dog Trixie barked sharply as he came closer in his black suit and began to climb the wide, steep steps. He climbed with purpose and concentration, looking up only when he came to the top of the steps.

I was expecting him, so he took off his coat, folded it, laid it on the swing beside him, with his Bible on top of it, sat down with me and greeted me formally, as usual, by shaking my hand. I had been to Vacation Bible School and still had on my blue cotton dress with the red flowers and white piqué collar. But I had taken off my sandals and was barefoot. This morning, the county paving crew in their big, yellow trucks spewing hot, black tar had been at work paving the graveled road that led from the main road to the church. They had warned us, going and coming, to walk on the sides, but, try as I might, I had stepped on the tar-covered gravel, and some of the tar and pebbles had stuck in my sandals. I didn't want Mother to see them.

I knew that he must wonder why my hand was so cold in the middle of July. But he smiled gently and opened up the small, pink catechism and asked if I was ready. I clasped the squeaky chain of the swing, nodded, and he began. I looked at his shiny, black shoes and recited.

The winter before, Mother had said it was about time to learn the catechism when she caught my sisters and me quarreling over a game of "set back." She came from the kitchen with wet, soapy hands when

43

someone yelled "cheater." It didn't take her long to see that the old, worn deck of cards had such distinguishable marks that it was easy to spot certain cards, and someone had turned down the corner of an ace. She yanked the cards out of our hands, opened up the front of the black, wood heater, and threw them in the fire. "It's a sin to argue over a card game," she said. "It's time you learned the catechism. There's no time like the present." So my sisters and I had memorized the answers to all the questions during the long, snow-filled days when school was called off because of icy side roads.

It was customary to say the catechism to your Bible School teacher on the last day of the two-week session and to receive, at the closing program, a New Testament, inscribed with your name, your teacher's name and the preacher's signature.

Earlier in the day, I had recited before my teacher, but I had gotten so nervous that she told the preacher maybe I should recite it again later. She believed I knew it, she said, but I seemed too distracted to justify her issuing a certificate. The preacher had studied me gravely and suggested that he come to my house later in the evening and give me another chance.

Now here he was in his white shirt and black tie sitting with me in the swing as I answered his questions.

"Who made you?"

"God."

"Why did God make you?"

"For His own glory."

"What must you do to have everlasting life?"

"Love God and keep His Commandments."

By the time we had gotten to the really hard answers in the back of the catechism, I was able to loosen my grip on the chain a little and to look at the preacher's face and to see, up close, the scar running across his right cheek. He had both feet on the porch with his elbows on his knees. He held the small book out in front of him. His eyes were pale, almost colorless, behind the gold, rimless glasses, and the part in his neat, short, almost-white hair was pink from the heat and looked as though it had been oiled.

Mother had said: "You watch out for him and be on the front porch waiting when he gets here. I'm going out in the garden."

The preacher and his wife visited often in the community and always on Sunday greeted everyone personally before church services began. With her gray-brown hair plaited neatly and wound around her head, a white shawl around her shoulders, summer and winter, and white gloves on her

44

tiny hands, the preacher's wife came from the front pew to greet everyone. She always wore black, lace-up shoes with sturdy heels and little designs punched out in the toes. The gold in her front teeth shone when she smiled. When they came to the home to visit, the preacher always helped her with her coat and shawl, and, when it rained, he helped her off and on with her galoshes.

When they came to visit us, we were always afraid of what Daddy might say. Sometimes he was outspoken and even short; they were always so formal, polite, and soft-spoken.

Daddy took us to church every Sunday and let us out, but he did not go in. Mother always said she did well to get us ready—hair combed, ears washed, patent leather shoes shined with the insides of a hot biscuit—much less herself.

The preacher closed his book, smiled at me and told me that I had done well, shook my hand again, and picked up his Bible and coat. As he walked down the steps, he reminded me that the commencement program began at 6:00 and that he was looking forward to seeing me there with my family for the program and the covered-dish supper that followed.

That evening, Daddy came home tired and sweaty. He shook the sawdust out of his overalls, threw down his thermos and lunch box, took out his ruler and laid it on his cap on the old piano, and, as usual, took a beer out of a small, brown paper bag.

"Where's supper?"

"We're going to Bible School Commencement—and it's Sister's birthday."

"Where's your mother?"

"She's out in the garden while we clean up and wash and get ready for tonight."

He went outside to the edge of the garden, and I poured water into the wash pan to drown out the loud voices.

Mother came into the house crying. "Are you all ready?" she said as she began to wash her dirty hands and to wipe the sweat out of her hair and off her face and the back of her neck.

Daddy muttered under his breath and went out on the front porch to cool while we finished getting ready.

He dropped Mother and us at the church and then went on down the road. The bell was ringing, and everyone was already in the church. We hurried up the rock steps and rushed into the back pew. Everyone's head was bowed, and the preacher was praying, his hand raised in the air. At the end of the prayer, as everyone began to sing "Jesus Loves Me" with the preacher directing, swinging his hymnal back and forth, he looked up, saw us, and smiled.

When the song was over, while the preacher gave his welcome, we scooted up the aisle to the front seats where our classes sat ready to present their parts of the program. Mother sat down in the back pew.

Afterwards, we went outside and were ready to leave when the preacher came through the yard to greet us. "Won't you stay for the supper?" he asked. Mother explained that we had not prepared anything, but he persisted, saying there was enough food for everyone, gesturing toward the rows of white-clothed tables lined with food under the shade tree. The Women of the Church had set everything up while the program was going on. He followed us out to Daddy's car where Daddy sat waiting, one arm slung across the back of the front seat. The preacher went to Daddy's side of the car and asked him to join in the fellowship.

"Preacher, I'm not cleaned up," Daddy said.

"That doesn't make any difference," the preacher said. "All of us need to fellowship together. There's no time like today. Won't you and your family please stay?"

I saw tears in the preacher's eyes and heard the urgency in his quiet voice. Daddy revved up the motor, and we tumbled into the back seat, falling over each other, grasping onto the back of the front seat.

"Maybe another time, Preacher," Daddy said.

"This may be our last time, Brother," the preacher said, and I saw the tears well up in his pale eyes again.

He was still begging us to stay as Daddy pulled out of the church yard. I looked back and saw him standing there watching us, a short, stocky figure in black, his Bible in his hand. When we got home, Daddy got out two bags. One had a Bost Bakery coconut layered cake in it. He had gone to the store while we were in church. The other bag had a six-pack with two missing.

After we had put six pink candles on the cake and lit them, Daddy insisted on saying the blessing. He had never done that before, and he weaved a little over the table and I smelled the warm beer on his breath. Sister hardly had enough breath to blow out the candles, and I had to force my piece of cake down with the lemonade we had made earlier.

Grandma was always saying that someday Daddy would come back to the fold. Bring up a child in the way that he should go and when he is old he will not depart from it, she would quote. I tried to imagine Daddy getting baptized as Grandma had said he had done when he was twelve years old. I saw him in his worn, gray suit, black tie, and white shirt only when he went to someone's funeral. I remembered this past winter when I was baptized. It had been snowing off and on for two or three weeks. The snow had crusted over and hardened and someone had dug a path to the church. The church was cold, and I had kept on my coat through the baptizing. When the preacher dipped his hand into a small, silver goblet of water and placed it on my head, I had felt the water run down my neck to the coat to my white blouse. After we got home, someone had taken my picture— a small figure lost in a heavy, winter coat in the white snow standing outside by the water pump to show how deep the snow was.

The preacher retired later that year, and we never saw him again. Mother always said she was sorry that we hadn't stayed that night when he asked us to. He must have known he was going to retire then, she said. He had watched us all grow up, and she was sorry that we hadn't stayed. There's no time like the present, she always said.

REUNIONS

Preacher

The river ran red with the preacher's blood. He bathed in it. It was warm and lulled him while the rushing waters launched him towards eternity. As he washed over the rocks, a spray of his own red blood created a halo of light around him. He floated, cradling his son in his useless arms. A beautiful white flower floated by, crimson-centered —his wife. Her white, stem-like arms held her face gracefully as she washed away, out of sight in the warm, red river of blood.

. . .

In a church as spare and sparse as its religion, the preacher strode, golden red hair aflame, a vision in a white suit, almost aglow with fervor and reverence. "He's in his glory," the old woman in the front row whispered to her companion, gripping her arm with a quivering, gloved hand.

. . .

"The bridge eased its footing. You know those old bridges, not made to withstand floods—the Lord, you know, never gives us more pain than we can bear—and the preacher's car went right into the river. Threw his young son out against a rock and killed him outright. His wife, too. They found her downstream a ways. Dead, too, pretty as a picture. Her dark hair had come down. They said she could sit on it when it was down."

. . .

Flush with the feel of Cathryn's shining hair in his hand and the soft, white sea of blossoms encircling them under the apple tree, the preacher fell into ecstasy.

. . .

"Young Cathryn's baby died. She shamed her family, having an outchild. Still they grieved. The preacher and his family paid their respects, prayed with them that fateful day."

. . .

Tommy, Cathryn's young beau, walked through the pasture, an air of insouciance about him, the sun catching on his shiny, new belt buckle. With the omnipotence of youth, he tied the bull he had come for to his new belt buckle and started home. From a distance, Tommy's mother saw Death coming in the form of a mad, snorting bull, dragging her son's beautiful body home, rivers of blood streaming behind him.

. . .

"Sure was a day for funerals. There were the preacher's wife and son, young Cathryn's infant daughter Grace, and Tommy. And the preacher rising out of that river, walking into the church, preaching all those funerals. Glory be!"

. . .

The day was dark, clouds overhead purple as a bruise. The preacher spurned his white suit forever for a dark one, and the old women touched him gently on his shoulder like a son.

Reunions

After food on the porch
lined with flower buckets
and straw-bottomed chairs
that moved with the sun,
children climbed on the island of rock
to play and pose.

I remember Grandma,
her eyes still keenly blue,
wondering about saving seed from the hollyhock.

I hear her remembering:
Grandpa cutting logs from around the rock
to build the house;

her children running naked
in the cane patch below the rock
once when they had the itch;

the burning of tobacco beds all night,
and young boys getting drunk for the first time
then getting sick and lying against the big, cool rock
until sunrise;

children playing church on the big rock,
singing old revival songs in high, quavery voices
in the twilight.

Grandma died last year,
and one Saturday afternoon when the sun had dropped
and moved invisible chairs to the last triangle of shade
on the front porch,

strangers set sticks of dynamite under the rock,
and, in the falling light, the big rock groaned
and then crumpled like a giant clod of dirt.

The sun's red glow died on the horizon
like the last coals of a burnt-out tobacco bed.

Pioneer Woman

Pioneer woman,
in all my silences
I think of you:

when the blue sky
cupped its wide expanse
over you,

when the deep nights
swallowed you
in fitful sleep,

when your hands
(worn from work)
searched for something to do,

when you waited
in a cold cabin
for a step, a cry—

a reason why.

Obituary

I watched you
die today

There was no noise
and nothing slightly personal

They just
wheeled you
out

looking rather doubtful
about
resurrection

Requiem

The land is silent and still.
The pale, sandy earth begs rain.
Tobacco stands in long, even rows,
leaves wilted like silken, green handkerchiefs.

He walks with his familiar gait,
legs slightly straddled,
hands crossed hard behind him,
staring intently at the ground.

He no longer wears his strange apparel,
his funeral garments.

His gray work shirt is darkened
by wings of sweat.
The legs of his blue, gallused overalls
rub against each other.

An errand, he says.

We walk around the road
bruised with beauty.

On the porch, her summer cactus still blooms
her favorite color.
She always wanted to be buried in red.

She lingers in the room
in her Spring Flowers perfume.

He fumbles among the stack of bills
stuck between the radio and the Bible.

Answers to the federal government he dictates
as I write:
His wife has died ....

I close the door behind me.

The oncoming roar of the usual afternoon shower
breaks the string in my mind;

the calm is shot by the sweetest sound
as the first drops begin to pound
the dry ground.

Funeral

The sun was so hot
even the plastic flowers looked wilted.

"Isn't it a lovely day for a funeral?"

The angry fist in my chest
beat against my best Sunday dress.

"I love the view from here."

. . .

Aunt Pallie is dead, Daddy said.
We went to pay our respects.

"She looks like she could speak."

I remember Uncle Jeff in a rocker,
his features stone, light catching on his bald head,

his bony hands moldy onion skin
with large, blue-black veins.

"He won't live long without her."

I sat on the bed near the casket
and wondered where Aunt Pallie's legs were.

White Lightning, Planes, and Such

He wore white bucks
and traveled light.

In a big orange bird
he took his flight.

He drank hard
and cut a rug in the sky.

People cried:
Hey, look at him fly,

flipping and zipping,
spitting fate in the eye.

He's over Vestal's now
putting on a show for the old folks,

cutting the motor in a free fall,
buzzing the telephone pole.

Stock-still they stood
in their yards

looking upward,
shading their eyes from the sun,

listening to the plane's drone
long after its Sunday afternoon ritual was done

and it had flown out of sight
over the hills towards home.

. . .

The dots on the ground elongate themselves
in quicksilver motions, pointing to the sky,

their bird-like mouths reaching for his golden glory
(they're on country ground; they can't rise).

One of these days he'll kill himself
without the thrill of white lightning, planes, and such—

he'll die like all of us,
without a fuss.

Come and rest, orange bird.
Come and shelter yourself.

Elegy

When he was tight
he loved to play
sweet music
on the piano
stomping his feet
hunching over the keys
concentrating almost violently
on the rhythm
head bobbing
sweat beginning
over words fumbled for

Then late
with the other misfits
who walked the roads with him
and fell drunk indiscriminately
he found a church
He moaned
old-timey hymns
and Hank Williams
his cronies
shivering around
his radiant wet face

He was just beyond thirty
when they raided the place
and put him out of business

DWELLING
PLACES

Forbidden Fruit

The heat bangs off the dark blue and white Humko lard buckets, and they screak as she swings them back and forth in either hand as she walks. Beyond the paved road, the now shaded, powder-dry path leads into the woods. She walks along the path until she comes to an opening leading to a meadow-like field. Eden-like, it is a new world filled with clumps of forbidden fruit, for this is government property. But the wild strawberries are ripe, and everyone knows that the park ranger is not at home in the morning.

The berries smell sweet and hang in heavy clusters. Their oblong shapes seem stretched to fullness leaving a slightly whitened neck under the cap. They are particularly large for wild strawberries, and she and her mother come here each year to pick them for fresh pies and jam. After cajoling and begging, she has persuaded her mother to let her come alone for just this one time. The earth is loamy, and the air is damply hot. Protected by their leaves and small, dry sticks, the berries are coated with a fine mist, like frost. It is immensely quiet, and the first berries fall with small thumps into the tin bucket as she picks, lifting the vines, being careful not to step on ripe berries as she moves from one corner of the field to the center. She fills one of the two gallon buckets and, except for an occasional twig snapping as she steps and a hummingbird whirring in sudden intervals, hears only the soft grass move under her feet. She no longer hears the intermittent, shrill cry and drone of the sawmill in the valley below.

She is hot now and sits under a tree at the edge of the patch. Her hat is wet, and, as she takes it off, some hair, lightened by the sun, falls around her neck. She sets the bucket of berries carefully on a flat rock in the shade of the tree. She pries the top off the other bucket, which she has left under the tree, and eats. The cornbread is fat and cold, and the onions are small and fresh, their tops stubby and green where they have been chopped off. She grinds them into a mound of salt which she has poured onto the bucket's lid from a piece of folded wax paper.

When she is finished eating, she smooths the remaining salt into a flat, round circle on the lid and scrawls her initials in it. Then she abruptly flings it away, dusts out the lid, claps her hands together to get rid of it, and jumps up. A small, pale-blue butterfly zigzags in her path and lights on the bucket of berries. She catches it and, holding it gently between thumb and forefinger, carries it away from the tree into the sun and throws it forward and upward. Fly away, little butterfly, she says and goes back for her hat and the now empty other bucket.

When the second bucket is filled, she turns from the silence of the field and the converging, small paths of parted vines and grass where she has picked. Her eyes catch the flash of red, like a bird, darting across the opening to the woods. She walks towards it. The red moves as she moves, suddenly filling up the opening. Unafraid, she continues to walk, her eyes fixing on a red shirt with sleeves rolled up over the elbows of brown arms then moving downward to blue work pants rolled at the top of hard, cracked boots. They are drawn upward again to the burst of red, then slowly to the eyes in the face above. She stops, turns and moves again towards the tree where she drops her bucket and sits propped against the trunk. From beneath the brim of her hat, she looks at the opening. She then lies down on her back and puts her hands under her head. A bird flaps its wings, and she looks up as it lights in a nest in the corner of the second branch above. In a moment, it flies again. She traces the branches in the sky above her. A cloud catches on one and appears to break into a head. The dismembered body floats away in the other direction. She floats on the cloud.

Suddenly a twig snaps, and she hears the soft grass moving. As her eyes turn to the field again, the red shirt moves. The body treads heavily through one of her paths, twigs snapping under the boots. She sits up again and feels him looking down at her. She closes her eyes and opens them again to meet his, intense and shining. She smiles and reaches her hand over to the side of her and offers him the juicy berry she has set on a small rock—the largest, the best of the lot, her souvenir. He bites into

70

it slowly, and she hears the sucking sound as he takes the juice from it. He finishes the berry while she watches, looking at him intently yet innocently, like a child. Then she gets up and straightens her hat, takes the two lard buckets, one in each hand, and starts walking away. He follows, looking puzzled. They both walk out of the forbidden place into the bright sun glaring off the small, shiny rocks on either side of the road. He rights a beat-up, dusty motorcycle and takes the two buckets and hangs one on each handlebar. He steers it through the path out of the woods. He hauls himself onto the machine and jumps it to life with the quick motion of one big, cracked boot. The cycle sputters, catches, and roars. He motions with his head for her to get on behind him. Unhesitatingly, she moves and holds on.

As they roar around the curve, off the graveled road, onto the pavement, she hears again the rasping drone of the sawmill, punctuated at precise intervals with a shrill whine as the saw moves through the logs.

About a mile down the road, she allows her head to rest on the red back as she sees the road suddenly long before them. But seconds later, she says "Here" at a clump of mailboxes with a few straggly petunias growing around them. He scrapes his boot on the pavement and comes to a stop. She gets off, and he hands her the buckets, looks at her for a moment, and revs up again. She watches him disappear into a tiny, black speck at the end of the long, straight expanse of road, the sound no longer loud but soft and muffled, reverberating in her head as she crosses the bridge leading home, swinging her berry-laden buckets.

Dwelling Places

It was on the lazy, warm summer nights during school vacation with the wet grass feeling so good to bare feet that they played hide and seek. Her once red-checkered shorts, now faded into white, smelling permanently of Clorox, and her yellow tee-shirt, now only faintly proclaiming the Great Smokies, were her summer uniform.

They were tearing down the old house and building a new one. She was saddened to see the old house go and to see the grape-like clusters of wisteria shrivel as the vine was torn from its clinging position. The family was staying up the road in Grandma's big house until the new one could be completed. (She had this recurring dream where she was walking barefoot, in her nightgown, back to the old house, back to the warmth of its familiar smells.)

He was helping her father. He came in the day while her father was at work. She watched his straight, brown back as he pried away the planks, his muscles straining with the crowbar. (One Sunday morning she dreamed his face floated from the foot of her bed where he was standing, and his smile loomed large as he leaned over and kissed her. She awakened, startled, not sure that she had been dreaming.)

One night as they played hide and seek, she slipped into the cool well house. She thought she was found out when suddenly he slipped in behind her as she crouched beside the freezer and she felt his own bare legs against hers. It seemed so natural and peaceful all at once—the square, cement dwelling with only a small window to let in light was set apart then from the world of cool, moonlit, dewy grass and the yellow light from the porch and the screaming of the other children. She leaned back in the circle of his arms and waited, now sure that they couldn't be found, when she felt his hands moving upward on her legs. Instinctively, she bolted forward and lunged for the door, ran around to the shadow behind the house and leaned back, feeling the roughness of the cement blocks holding her up. Then he was there, too. Don't tell anyone what I did, he said, his voice too loud and too deep. She realized they'd never talked alone before—no conversations take place during grass fights. You didn't do anything, she said, and then ran to steal "home."

Whenever they played hide and seek again, she always sat on the porch or just inside the screen door reading his comic books. The others taunted her for a while but soon lost interest as they played.

Always shy and always a good reader, she now began to read more and more. She read a dusty novel she got from the bookmobile about a young girl who disguised herself as a Confederate soldier whose identity was not discovered until she was wounded and the tall captain stripped the blood-soaked uniform from the frail, unconscious body. She no longer liked the yellow, threadbare tee-shirt and the faded shorts.

It was the end of the summer, and the old house was now torn down. She watched with wonder as the new house's shape was formed with stakes and twine, as the footing was dug and the cement blocks laid, as subflooring was hammered into a foundation, and as the walls and roof were raised. After dark, she wove in and out of the skeletal rooms, playing with her shadow and those of the two by fours. This strange, box-like structure was still a puzzle—a maze, a novelty to be tried on. Yet, she liked the smell of the new wood.

Work on the house was slow in the winter, and the skeleton stood in its black tarpaper siding. That winter as they stood in the cold—stiffly silent, mittened, booted, waiting for the school bus—she looked at his crisp, brown hair and white, even rows of teeth, but not when he looked her way. She trembled a little (not just from the cold) and felt funny breathing. Her mouth was dry, and she wasn't sure anything would come out if she were forced to speak.

The following spring, they ran the sheetrock and painted the walls. The hardwood floors were laid and shellacked. She took old rags and slid barefoot across their shining surfaces, and the smell of the new wood was only a memory. One day he came back to admire her father's handiwork and to talk to him about getting his own car. (He smiled at her impersonally.) She realized with a shock that he was taller than her father, who had always looked like such a giant to her.

Twice a week that summer her family got milk from his family since their cow was dry, and his family had a fresh one. One Saturday she crossed the bridge with a gallon jar under each arm, went to the back screen door, and knocked as usual. She handed the jars to his grandmother and waited for her to pour one full when he suddenly came through in his underwear looking for breakfast. When he saw her, he turned and ducked quickly out of the room. His grandmother laughed a little.

She saw him a few more times that summer—not for grass fights; he was driving and dating now. She saw him at church, inaccessible in the back row, and, once, about three years later, after he had graduated and joined the army, he came to see her father, looking even taller and more remote in his uniform. He nodded to her as he swept by.

Dinosaur

I first saw him on the Saturday after my fourteenth birthday, but I had heard a lot about him that summer. He had set up an open-air market called Pearl's Poetry Parlor (which I thought was an interesting play on words) where he also cut hair and read poetry over a loudspeaker. People said that he used to teach in some college but that now he was as crazy as a loon. (That next school year, whenever the bully of the school wanted to ridicule someone, he called him "Pearlie.")

The proprietor of Pearl's Poetry Parlor was Jeffrey Pearl—his patrons called him "Professor." Prof. Pearl sold everything. My aunt, who was also to be my teacher in the fall when school began, read religiously the newsletter that he put out each week. Besides advertisements for all the merchandise he carried, he also offered services such as poetry critiques.

Since my aunt fancied herself a poet, she clipped the ad, and, early one Saturday morning, we set out for Prof. Pearl's. She had taken me under her wing for the summer since I was to be her pupil in the fall and since my mother was working overtime in the factory in town. She had given me the literature textbook to read which I went through in one night. I didn't tell *her* so. I made a great show of reluctance, but I loved all the stories and the poems. She insisted also that I begin to keep a journal which I did, balking outwardly at the idea. After all, I did have a reputation to maintain—that of a wisecracking tomboy, smart alecky and self-sufficient. I took great delight in second-guessing my aunt, so I kept one for her and one for me.

My aunt was an old maid—everyone said, but not to her face. Nonetheless, she was really sensitive about the matter and lectured us all about it.

But the title really fit, and it was hard not to think of her in those terms. She was also very close with the penny—people said she was so tight she screaked—and wanted to be sure that she always got her money's worth. I guess she felt that she could get a crash course in the art of poetry for $1.95 if she took her poems to the professor.

That Saturday morning she stopped by to get me on her way to the market. After lecturing me on the evils I would find there—drunken men and loose women—she told me to look out for some good tomatoes and squash, instructing me completely and lengthily in the art of buying good produce. I sat in the back seat nodding my head, trying to appear only appropriately interested when she looked in the mirror at me. I was really excited and impatient to get there.

After the rather long drive—my aunt was a very careful driver—we passed the homemade sign indicating that Pearl's Poetry Parlor was just ahead. I heard the music and voice before my aunt stopped the car in the parking lot. It was really just an open field with the market in the middle.

We got out, and I inched away as soon as I saw my aunt examining pink, plastic flamingos and began to make my way through the crowd to the front of the market where the professor was cutting hair and reciting to the accompaniment of a record player into a mouth-level microphone rigged up to the back of the barber's chair.

At first glance, the professor looked like a boxer. His head was massive, and he was overweight, but in a very muscular way. His hair was greasy, and his dingy, white shirt was wet with sweat. I elbowed closer until I was on the front row to his left, my tennis shoe propped against an ornately carved bedstead. I tried to look casual, but his voice excited me. It was mellifluous yet full-bodied, hard yet soft around the edges. When he finished a line, he looked over at me and caught my eye. I lifted one eyebrow in a challenging "Oh, yeah?" and jammed my hands further into my pockets. But I was impressed! His eyes, long-lashed, rich brown, despite the red lines, were expressive. The space in which he was working was very small and cluttered, and, when he finished, I felt his breath on my bare arm. He looked at me again and I shrugged. He smiled and showed strong, even teeth, stained, perhaps, from tobacco. I made my way back into the crowd a little and continued to observe him without his noticing me. He was supposed to be twenty-eight or thirty, which was old to me, but he looked older, lines already deep in his dark forehead where his greasy, curly hair tumbled now as he bent to concentrate on cutting hair once again. His arms, weather-tanned to where he rolled his sleeves, were big and hairy; his hands, large but beautifully shaped. He reminded me a little, at that moment, of an unkempt Clark Gable.

I made my way to the produce and was assiduously examining tomatoes and squash when my aunt appeared again. "Let's sit down," she said, "until the crowd thins out. Then I want you to take my poems to the professor."

As noon approached, the crowd thinned to sparse, and my aunt carefully counted out $1.95 from her small, worn change purse. She handed me a sheaf of poems in a neatly labeled folder along with the money, admonishing me not to lose either.

Again, I made my way to the front. The professor was sweeping hair into a little pile in the corner of the dirt floor. He propped his broom up and sat down in the battered barber's chair. I swaggered forward and thrust the folder and money to him in one gesture. He took them in his big hand.

"These yours?" he asked in his deep voice.

"No, they're my aunt's over there," I said, jerking my thumb over my shoulder, indicating my aunt in one of the rickety chairs at the edge of the arena.

"Come back next Saturday, and I'll have them ready for you," he said.

I nodded and started to walk away.

"Liked my poetry, eh?" he added.

I stopped and spun around defensively, but he was smiling. I walked on.

When I got back to my aunt, she had three or four tomatoes and two or three squash picked out. "Now, Honeybunch, go and get these and we'll leave," she said.

I gritted my teeth and smiled. Now I had to walk all the way back up there and watch him look through me again.

When I got back up to him in his chair, he was drinking a bottle of orange soda. He got up and set his drink down next to the dusty cash register beside the barber tools on the small, makeshift desk. "How about a cold drink?" he said as he rang up the produce, put the change in the drawer, and handed me the tomatoes and squash in a crushed-up bag he fished from a disheveled mound inside the desk.

"No, thanks," I answered coolly.

"Okay, suit yourself," he said and smiled again.

How come I could fool everybody but him, I wondered, as I made my way to the car where my aunt sat waiting.

When we returned the next Saturday, I noticed four children playing with a huge, taffy-colored dog in the field where we parked. Rumor was that the professor had two children of his own and that two more had just wandered in and stayed. As I got out of the car (my aunt having mysteriously decided to pick up her poems herself from the professor), I looked at the children more carefully. They were all very dirty for it had rained the night before, and they were playing in the mud puddles created in the field by the tire tracks. Their clothes were nondescript and mostly brown now from the mud. I picked out the two that looked like him. They were chubby and stout with dark, unruly curls all over their heads—one boy and one girl. The other two, also one boy and one girl, were skinny as sticks with thin, stringy blond hair.

"What's his name?" I asked as I sidled up to them, indicating the dog.

"Taffy," they answered in unison, looking up from their mud pies.

"Where's your mama?" I asked.

The two curly headed ones looked at each other for a few minutes, sharing a secret, then continued to play. The other two skinny ones just looked blank as they patted daisies into their cakes. I sat on a rock and petted Taffy.

After a while, one of the stout ones looked up from where he sat on his haunches and spoke. "My daddy reads palms," he said.

I nodded, looking impressed, leaning forward conspiratorially.

"He read Taffy's paw," the other one giggled.

I laughed and said good-by as they were getting ready to eat their pies and wandered into the arena and looked around. Sure enough, there was a hand-lettered sign above the cloudy mirror behind the barber's chair. "Palm Reading," it said. I milled around and saw my aunt in a chair poring over her poems. I found my familiar spot beside the bedstead again and listened raptly. The professor looked up and saw me, smiled, and continued to recite.

When he was finished, he turned in my direction and bowed with a great flourish, I felt my skin begin to redden. I was glad my aunt was oblivious to these goings-on.

On the way home, my aunt wanted to know why I was so quiet. "I'm thinking about my journal," I said. "The Parlor would make a good subject." I persisted. "By the way, what did the professor say about your poems?"

Now it was her turn to redden and squirm a little. "What does he know about poetry, anyway?" she sniffed. "That place is dirty and coarse—no place for womenfolk to be." Subject closed. I knew this was the end of our trips there, but I vowed to myself that I would find a way to go back.

The next Saturday morning when my aunt called on me and wanted me to go with her to the schoolhouse to dust the seats and chalkboard in preparation for the fall opening—she liked to prepare for everything in advance—I feigned illness. She felt of my head and pronounced a summer cold. "Go back to bed, Precious, and get plenty of rest. You want to be well when school starts."

As soon as she was out of the driveway, down the road and out of sight, I jumped on my bike and headed for Pearl's Parlor.

It was noon when I reached the edge of town. I parked my bicycle under a tree and headed for my familiar spot. The professor was finishing his recitation, but something was lacking. His voice seemed flat and dull. When he finished, he looked up, spotted me, and smiled apologetically, the bravura gone, the eyes lackluster. Something was wrong. I knew it. Then suddenly I remembered my conversation with his children last week. I looked outside where they had been playing. Only the two blond, skinny ones were there now with Taffy. Just then, the crowd let out a gasp, and I looked back to the stage. The professor was sprawled on the dirt floor, his head resting at a strange angle against the bottom of the barber's chair. It was very clear to me, somehow, that he was dying. I burst forward from the crowd and was at his side. The crowd melted away, and, in my mind, it was as though only the two of us were there. I knelt down and took the massive head in my lap. "I wanted you to read my palm," I heard myself saying to him.

He smiled, and those eyes cleared again one last time. He looked knowingly at me. I heard his voice, full again, gently teasing, the bravura returning. "That's only for the children among us," he said, gesturing expansively with those great hands.

"I love you, you old dinosaur," I said, but he was already gone, expelling a great, last breath.

Maribelle and Co.

They called him Maribelle's love child, and, they say, a love child is always beautiful, isn't it?

He wore his beauty carelessly. One day in hot, scowling August, he rode his cycle over a fence into a neighbor's prize bull, and its horn followed the gentle curve of his cheek in a very clean-cut half moon so that afterwards, when he smiled, the thin line of the scar moved with his cheek and was barely noticeable. Nevertheless, his perfection was marred.

He was conceived, they said, in one of the small Sunday School rooms adjoining the sanctuary with the fading, solemn face of the first preacher brought in to civilize them looking gravely down from the wall.

The event took place, they say, after the annual Christmas pageant which was put on by the young people's group of the church.

Maribelle had the rather plain, earnest face which the group leader said would provide a good Mary when she cast her thus. With her brownish hair down from its customary ponytail and her rather longish face shining as she looked upward into the spotlight (in reality, a flashlight held in the first row with a square of blue cellophane over it) as the Magnificat was being read, she was, indeed, affecting.

The father was one of the Wise Men. As they came down the aisle bearing "gold, frankincense, and myrrh" (one of the girls' jewelry boxes, an ornately-cut bottle of cheap bubble bath, and someone's slightly tarnished gold-plated ashtray, respectively), they wore borrowed scarves, set askew on top of their flattops, their loafers and white socks protruding as they strode grimly forward in their fathers' striped bathrobes. Because he had forgotten his costume, one Wise Man, as a last resort, was obliged to wear the group leader's pink chenille robe obtained after a frantic trip to her house which happened to be next to the church.

From her draped, blue sheets, Maribelle cast her eyes solemnly on them as they, one by one, presented their gifts and then knelt before the manger. She held the eyes of the first Wise Man, who presented the "gold," a second or so longer and seemed to stare deeply into them.

(In rehearsal, everyone had been inclined to giggle but had kept poker faces as all the lights were switched off and the white candles lit in each window, warming the pieces of pine that encircled each one, releasing spicy smells. Shadows flickered from the one suspended light with a papier-mâché star around it—a huge, multi-faceted geometric design that the group leader had made out of white construction paper and glitter as a home ec. project when she was in school.)

When it was all over, they had gone back to the Sunday School rooms where the angels had unpinned their wings (shaped from two coat hangers covered with crepe paper and outlined with tinsel) and taken off their white sheets. The Wise Men had removed their scarves and robes, and Maribelle had unpinned her blue sheets. They then had all gone across the road to the fellowship hall for hot chocolate prepared by the group leader. They had played "Spin the Bottle," but, when the boys got a little rowdy, the group leader had suggested they go home. It was then, they say, that Maribelle and the Wise Men had gone back to the Sunday School room, lit only by the moon hitting on the stern face in the frame on the wall.

Maribelle continued in school that year, had the baby the following September, and was able to enroll a week late the following school year. She was also able to help the church group with the annual Halloween party, making huge candied apples which everyone said reminded them of the baby's pink cheeks.

By Christmas of that year, everything seemed back to normal. Once again, Maribelle made a glowing Mary, and, since the baby's father also continued to come to the church group, the group leader decided that the most natural thing to do was to promote him to the part of Joseph.

Maribelle graduated with her class and went on to become a practical nurse. The baby's father went into trucking to see the world but, after years of traveling all over the United States, came home to stay, declaring that he could find no place more beautiful than the place where he was born and raised.

84

Many Christmas eves later, he and Maribelle sat in the same pew at the church's annual pageant. Their son was now a Wise Man, and the delicate half-moon of the scar smoothed to a barely perceptible line as his smile widened into a large grin when he walked down the aisle and looked into the new Mary's shining face.

The Disappearance of Children

She had known before that last night with him that her family and his would celebrate his son Matt's birthday together the next day. He had been her father's best friend since high school, and they had celebrated each new year of their children's lives together.

He had ceased to be simply her father's best friend and had become hers also when he had given her a small, wooden top one Christmas. (Along with the top, he had included a small, signed, framed painting of it.) It was something special, unique among her other gifts. He had painted on the continents in red, white, and blue and marked their town with a tiny star. He had carved it carefully, shaping it to spin for the longest time. He started it for her the first time and was as delighted as she by the smoothness and swiftness of its turns, and, together, they watched the world spin before their eyes. Down on the floor beside him, their faces almost touching, she felt the warmth of his breath as he laughed and talked, and, when she had impulsively reached out to hug him, he had lifted her up and swung her around like the top.

She remembered also the time that he had ceased to be her best friend and had become something more—something not so definable. It was Easter, and they were all hiding eggs in the backyard. One of the older boys had decided to go beyond the agreed-upon bounds of the yard and had said she was "hot" when she had looked towards the corn crib.

She was still wearing her new white dress, white socks, and patent leather shoes as she slipped into the crib and began to climb up the side to look into the bird's nest on the rafters. Then, attempting to climb higher, she had placed her fingers into another crack in the planks and raised her foot to put her toe into another. The bottoms of the new shoes were still slick, and her foot suddenly slipped. She tried to catch herself, but her fingers could not hold her, and she slid down the side, desperately grasping for something to hold on to. She caught on an inside plank, nailed diagonally for support between the two by fours. About that same time, she felt a sharp, tearing pain in her wrist and remembered why children weren't supposed to climb in the crib. Her father hung his tools on the wall. Holding on to the plank, she looked down and saw bright red splotches spreading down the entire left side of her new white dress. She had brought her wrist down onto the teeth of her father's cross-cut saw that he had wedged, cutting edge upward for safety, inside the plank. Stiffly, she clung there, sucking in her breath, looking at the jagged pieces of flesh that the sharp teeth had flayed, watching the blood spurt until she heard the wooden latch on the door lift, and he was somehow there lifting her down and wrapping his clean, pressed handkerchief around her wrist. Not crying, she had stood quietly and obediently as he tied the ends together, the blood already seeping through. Then he touched her cheek and gently but firmly raised her chin and looked into her face. She looked into his eyes, feeling dizzy but not afraid. She let out her breath in a single sigh. He lifted her up and carried her out of the crib, her bandaged left arm hanging stiffly over his right shoulder, the blood on her dress oozing into the front of his white shirt.

Later, when it was all over, everyone had talked in hushed tones about the fact that the cuts had just missed the main artery and that she would have bled to death had it been severed. The bandages had to be changed frequently, and she would let only him change them for the gauze sometimes stuck to the wounds, and she was terrified that they would open up again as the bandages were pulled away. She believed that only his hands could work the magic necessary to keep them intact, and never once did the wounds open up as he gently removed the bandages, applied the medication, and put on new ones. It stung a little as he pulled the tape away, taking the short, golden hairs from her arm with it, but she stood mutely, unmoving, as his agile hands—the same ones that had carved and spun the top and touched her cheek—moved swiftly and surely. She studied him closely during those times, memorizing every line and plane of his face— when it was immobile and filled with concentration, when it was relaxed and smiling, when it was looking directly at her.

It was three months before her eleventh birthday when the accident happened, and, during those three months, she had been afraid to go to the corn crib. On her birthday, after the cake and presents, he had taken her hand (there was only a small bandage on her wrist now) and led her to the crib. Everyone except him had acted casual and kept on talking. He looked intent and serious. At the door, he asked her to lift the latch, and they entered together. Again, the familiar, musty smell of corn greeted her as did a new smell—the smell of blood and fear. She felt her stomach close up and nausea begin, and she realized that she was digging her nails into his hand. He released her hand, and, with both of his, carefully lifted the saw down from its diagonal resting place, and, reaching across its span, holding it by both handles, he held it in front of her, its teeth eye level with her. She looked at them, and, lifting up the arm with the bandage, she touched one sharp tooth. He returned it to its safe place, and they left the crib. After that, she went, as she had before the accident, into the crib for corn to shell for the chickens.

Soon a year had passed, and she was twelve and suddenly grown up. One summer evening while her family and his were sitting on the porch watching the lightning bugs shut off and lazily turn on again in the muggy air and the jagged streaks of lightning make giant, red, misshapen balloons out of the clouds, someone suggested that they make some ice cream. She went with him across the road to his garage to look for the churn while the boys went for ice, and some of the others went into the kitchen to mix the ingredients.

The garage was his creation. Its ceiling was blue with four or five pale, white stars painted on. On the cement blocks, halfway up either side of the garage, were recognizable peaks of the Blue Ridge painted in bold shades of purple. The rest of the way up was painted blue with puffy, white clouds. On the front wall, the wall that the car faced, was a portrait of the artist —his self-portrait—sitting in front of an easel, painting the scene before him, the view from his own front yard. The floor of the garage was green. At the base of the closed garage door, one could look back at a bright, neon sun. This was his world, and, although he never sold any of his paintings, he did give away a few. Many of the others stood propped against the walls of the garage in various stages of completion.

While he looked for the churn, he opened the car door and turned on the radio. She sat on the driver's side while he searched among clinking bottles and cans and buckets and brushes, her bare feet dangling on the green concrete outside. The music was soft, and suddenly he was there before her. He set down the churn, bowed, and stretched out his arms towards her in a mock invitation. She reached out, and he pulled her up out of the seat and into his arms. They danced silently around the small, clear area inside the open car door, her toes barely reaching the concrete now, making no sound, his crepe-soled canvas shoes, a barely perceptible squeak now and then as they pivoted to change directions. When the song was over and the deejay came on with a spot for Lucky Strikes before announcing the next song on the Hit Parade, he still held her. Just as his lips grazed her forehead, she felt the side of the car against her leg, cool and smooth. They're waiting for us, she said, surprised at her own voice.

Over the next year, they had met many times in the garage. Sometimes she just watched him paint, and sometimes they sat in the car and talked about the dreams he had had when he was a young boy and of hers. During these times, she always had the feeling that she was talking to someone far removed from the person who came with a family. It was as though he were her own age and they were growing up together, less painfully and more knowledgeably than they ever could separately. She was enchanted, and he was patient and she loved him more than a friend, better than a brother, and more intensely than a father.

That night before his son's birthday, he had been more reflective and somber, perhaps, she thought much later, because his last child was getting older and his own age was intruding more persistently. She thought that she smelled alcohol on his breath when his face brushed hers, and she was puzzled when she heard him cry out as she hugged him quickly before she gathered her things and left.

At the celebration the next day, after the cake and the ice cream, everyone except his wife, who insisted on finishing the dishes alone, went out under the big shade tree in the front yard with a chair. He and her father played a game of softball with all the children until everyone began to pant and to call for a rest. They all sprawled on the grass in the shade.

Eventually, Matt began to climb trees and ended up in an apple tree where he sat throwing green apples towards the group. They bantered with him for a while, indulging him on his birthday, his father only gently scolding him about the gastronomical dangers inherent in eating green apples.

Soon the group began a half-hearted game of tag, and Matt's father was chasing her. Just as she grabbed around a tree, he tagged her. Out of breath,

90

they leaned against each other. She heard his racing heart and flashed back to the night before. Instinctively, she looked up, catching his eyes, wanting somehow to rescue him as he had her two years ago, though not really understanding why or from what. Just then, someone screamed, and, somewhere in her peripheral vision, she caught sight of his wife, coming out of the house, her face white. Then she saw Matt and everyone looking up at him. Matt's face was purple, his eyes bulging as he clung, immobile, to a branch in the tree. Suddenly his father was no longer beside her but was rushing to pull Matt from the tree. The screams of the other children reverberated in her ears. He's choking! He's choking! His father swung him down from the tree with both hands, and, in one swift motion, turned him upside down with one hand and began to beat him on the back with the other. Matt hung limply in his green and white striped shirt, and the anguish in his father's face told her all she needed to know.

Everyone stood back a little then and watched him as he tried vainly to breathe life into the small body, now beneath him on the grass. A jarfly sang—the only noise, suddenly amplified in the quiet.

Finally, his father got up, and she noticed, distractedly, some grass stains on one of his rolled-up sleeves. He bowed his head and walked toward the house, passing his wife silently. Falling to the ground, she reached outward for her son, clasping him to her, his arms dangling beside her.

The funeral was a horrible affair with Matt's parents sitting stiffly together, neither reaching out to the other for comfort.

She sat between her parents. Matt was dead, and she wanted to tell him she was sorry, sorry for taking his father away.

Later, as he sat beside the grave, she wanted to go to Matt's father and to put her arm around his shoulder and tell him it wasn't his fault and lead him to the casket, cool, smooth, and shiny, and have him touch it and see it open suddenly and see Matt step out in his tee shirt and his tow-headed smile, but she knew that he would only take her by the hand and lead her to the casket and place her hand on its cold, gray surface before the attendants, surely and safely, with a lifetime of practice, lowered it into the dark, patient earth.

Jealousy

"The heart is the toughest part of the body.
Tenderness is in the hands."
—Carolyn Forché

It is Monday—washday. Last night it had rained only enough to wet the dry ground and make it steam. She had knelt in the dark in front of the open, screenless window and listened to the first drops hitting the leaves of the maple tree outside, the smell of dirt in her nostrils. She had prayed that it would rain all night—one of those soft, steady rains that drum on tin roofs and lull one into an everlasting sleep. She had wanted to sleep through washday anyway. But after the shower had dropped its first big plops on the leaves, it had stopped, and she had prayed where she was in her still-kneeling position before the open window and asked God to forgive her selfishness, for she knew if the washing did not get done on Monday the work would only pile up for the rest of the week, and she and her mother would have to work even harder to catch up.

But today the sun is out, and she wonders if Billy will come. She dreads to see him. She doesn't know if she can face him after everything that's happened. Billy is everyone's handyman while he himself lives alone in a ramshackle old house nearby. He always comes by on washdays to help out. She carries water from the pump outside and fills up the big tin tub on the wood stove in the kitchen. When the water is boiling, she helps her mother lift the tub off the stove and carry it to the Maytag wringer washer in the corner of the kitchen. Then, listening to the sloshing of the agitator, she begins the cycle again—going in and out, filling and refilling the two tin buckets until the tub on the stove is full again.

Billy usually arrives in time to help her carry out the tubs of dirty, ropey wash water when the first load is finished. Sometimes, as the clothes are rinsing, she cooks dinner for him, her mother, and herself. They all carry their plates into the living room to cool off and turn on the radio and listen to "Helen Trent" and "Our Gal Sunday" while they eat.

After dinner, her mother runs the clothes through the wringer, puts in another load to wash in the rinsing water, and goes out to hang the clothes on the clothesline while she begins to refill the tub on the stove—this time with Billy's help.

Washing clothes is an all-day task, and, when they have carried out their last tub of dirty water and poured it into the branch by the side of the house, she and Billy go through their ritual, swinging the tub high in the air between them, throwing it to the ground, and sinking down beside it with sighs of relief, resting for a while on the cool grass.

Today they are more than halfway through, and still Billy has not come. She and her mother work in silence. She is tired but relieved. She cannot look directly at her mother's face. She thinks instead about Billy. She cannot remember a time when he hasn't been around. When she was very small, he minded her while her mother picked blackberries in the pasture, canned peaches, or chased someone's cows out of the garden. They sat in the swing out on the front porch or took chairs out beside the house in the sun. When she was very tired or sleepy, she sat in Billy's lap and rested her head against the Prince Albert can in the bib of his overalls. It was during those times that she imagined him her father. (Her father worked at the sawmill and cut timber. He was gone with his lunch bucket before she got up, and when he came home at night, he was too tired to do anything but eat and go to bed. Her mother often cautioned her to be quiet when he was home because he didn't want to be bothered; he needed his rest, she said.)

She remembers other times. Once, when her mother was putting up onions in the barn loft to dry out, Billy came by and helped her lift up the heavy basket. "All that work'll make an old woman out of a new one," he said. Mother blushed and turned it off, but she thought her mother had liked the attention.

Then she remembers back one Christmas when Billy had gone to town with her mother and father. (Since it was a long trip and one not made very often, she had stayed with one of the neighbors.) Billy looked stiff and uncomfortable in his ill-fitting, brown suit. She remembers now that that is the only time she has ever seen him in anything other than an oversized pair of denim overalls or a pair of gray or blue work pants and matching workshirt. He came in holding his hat—the same one he always wore—a gray felt one with a circed sweatband—and stood in the middle of the living room, holding out first one hand and then the other to the heater, shifting the hat from one hand to the other as he warmed and waited. Her father was dressed in his dark suit and white, starched shirt that her mother had ironed with the flat iron being careful not to scorch the collar. When her mother had entered the room, she wore her only suit, a rust and white checkered wool. A little black hat with a rolled-up veil sat on her hair which she had swept away from her face into rolls on either side. The scene was strange but nice also, for it was one of the few times that she had seen her mother dressed up.

In the car, they all had sat together in the front seat trying to stay warm —her father driving, her mother in the middle, Billy on the other side holding her in his lap for the short drive to the neighbor's house. She had stood on the running board a second after she got out, her breath taken from her in little milky-white clouds as she said good-by. She was sad as they pulled out of the icy, dirt road in the small, black, humpbacked car. They looked like a picture from a book, waving back, smiling at her as they disappeared down the road, the sun glancing off the car.

Then she remembers the time earlier this summer, when Billy helped them with the scarecrow, the one he put up in the upper field of corn to keep away the crows. First, he took two tobacco sticks and nailed them into a T-shape. "Bring me one of your daddy's old shirts—a bright one if you have it—and one of his old caps, and some twine." He draped the shirt over one of the sticks, stuck the cap in the other one, and tied them on with twine. He then carried the scarecrow to the middle of the field where he nailed it into the ground with a flat rock. "There she is," he said. "Only a tolerable one, but she'll do."

That night when her daddy came home from hauling pulpwood and went to the sink to wash up in the washpan, he saw the scarecrow through the window. He looked at it for a long time before he turned around, shaking his hands, slinging drops of water onto the stove where they sizzled and disappeared. Her mother stood very quietly at the table, cutting the steaming cornbread into crispy squares. "I suppose Billy put that up," he finally said.

Suddenly, like the sun shining on the frosty car that Christmas, her memory flashes back to something that had begun this past Saturday night. Unlike the first memories which are odd little aches now, this new one smarts. Still, she picks at it warily as she works. On Saturday night, her father had returned from hauling a load of logs. Supper wasn't quite ready, and he said something sharp. As usual, one thing led to another, and suddenly he had hit her mother, a swift, hard blow to the face that was so quick she didn't have time to look up from her plate and see it. But she heard it and heard her mother cry out sharply and run into the other room. She and her father had eaten their meal in silence. She was no longer hungry but was afraid to leave the table. (Her father left and didn't return that night. But he came in Sunday night as they knew he would, after the rain, and, once again, left for work this morning, their washday, carrying his old, black lunch bucket, as usual.)

It is another memory, yesterday's, that she struggles with now. On Sunday morning she had heard voices and had crept out of bed to the almost-closed door of the kitchen when she saw them. Her mother was sitting in a chair in front of the wood stove, where she had lit the shredded paper and kindling, waiting for the fire to catch up. She had on her faded, chenille robe. Billy was there also, kneeling beside her, an old man cradling her swollen cheek in his square hands, just looking at her. In the stillness of the room, Billy and her mother formed a sort of tableau, both of them remote and inaccessible to her. Her heart had turned over at the sight of them there, but she was also angry and inexplicably jealous. She had wanted to scream, to make them look away from each other—to her. She was immediately ashamed, and the scream died somewhere deep inside of her, and she had gone, barefoot and shivering, back to bed.

These memories carry her along, and, when the last pieces of clothing have been flung on the lilac bushes and the spreading arms of the maple, the clothesline having no more room, Billy still has not come.

Just as she and her mother are emptying the last tub of water into the branch, the preacher's car drives up. "They've taken Billy to the hospital," he says.

For the first time today, she looks at her mother. Her mother speaks first. "Preacher, if you'll wait ..."

The hospital corridor is long and narrow. The shiny, newly-waxed tile, looking almost transparent, swims in front of her. She looks at her mother. Her mother pushes her a little, indicating that she should go on ahead. "I'll stay here," her mother says, motioning towards a bench.

She isn't sure at all that she can walk down the hall to Billy's room, but somehow she does. The door to the room is open, and she sees him there, his arms sticking through his hospital gown, looking a little like the scarecrow he made for the cornfield. He motions towards her, and she kneels before his bed so that he can see her better. Tears well up in her eyes, and, when she looks at him, his face becomes all scrunched up and out of shape like when she looks at herself in the cheap, wavy mirror over the sink that her daddy shaves in. Billy looks at her for a long time. "You're looking more like your mama every day," he says.

Despite her best efforts, the tears spill out the corners of her eyes, run down her face, and into her mouth as Billy's face dissolves before her. "Everybody says so," she says.

SOME
TRAVELING
MUSIC,
PLEASE

Some Traveling Music, Please

You sit on your side
marking your territory,
one arm thrown carelessly out the window,
resting on the rolled-down glass,
the other barely touching the steering wheel,
moving it magically.

I admire your profile,
tough, brown, and handsome,
but I wouldn't want to say so.
I've learned that much about you:
You'd rather things were left unsaid
and, sometimes, consider talking a slight.

I suppose I like that about you—
one doesn't have to shout;
still, given half the chance,
I'd like to have your eyes linger
rather than glance.

A little traveling music, babe, you say.
I flip on the radio,
and forward we fly
into the darkness together
as night settles.

Skydiving

Free-falling
through life
is too easy

I'd rather float
with a discerning eye
earning my eternity

than to arrive
surprised
in paradise

White Petunias

You open like old dreams
mouthing double wishes.

Oozing sweetness,
veined throat straining,
pushing towards perfection,

you are an explanation for the night,
a definition of day breaking.

Yet, as you glow,
your fragrance forces some exploration
by bird or bee or foe,

and, already, the heat
is dancing in the street
with a vengeance,

inviting you to go.

Compromise

I started liking apple blossoms
that one day in April
when the lilacs got killed again
for the I-don't-know-how-many years in a row.

I had stopped counting by then.
Childlike, I figured they must be delicate or just too eager.

So I found that bright, blown morning
with the smell of lilacs a sweet memory
and the sugary spiciness of apple blossoms hitting,
that they could serve me well.

They endure.

Hack off limbs and doggedly they return next year
with new green sprouting
in the most unlikely, unbalanced places.

They are safe,
and I break armfuls in my quest

and leave mangled
up and down free forms
for the sun to shine hard upon.

Small Baptisms

Another flyer from the Golden Gate Bridge today . . .

The announcer,
dispassionate,
rises out of the radio
into the warm order
of the white tile.

I see a halo of orange steel over a still, black waterway.

I fall,
wide-eyed,
Icarus in nightgown,
a golden mote
caught in the sun's red eye.

I flow down to dark comfort.

Weather, he says,
nice, mild, calm today,
no wind (to speak of),
week-end storm
on the way.

Morning streaks
my shadow
on the wall—
pale double
hovers.

The announcer intones the time; day's duties call.

I bend to bathe
sleepy eyes:
I believe
in small baptisms
after all.

Elvis

We search
for you in all
the green mornings

You step out
of the fog
to greet us

Lush eyes
lusting hungrily
you drift towards us

heart drumming
dripping in black leather
as the sun comes up

To Zelda

Zelda
in your dancing shoes

why couldn't you choose
your way to die
in the sweet summer's sunset?

Why couldn't you
let the end come
and pick it like a choice plum

from the off-limits tree
that grew in the shining pool
with roots in the sky?

Home

Late in the day,
I go to pick roses,

their red marking
the cornerstones
of a house that used to be,

their dark fragrance
mingling with the dusky twilight....

Voices stir.

A certain strongness
settles in my bones.

I respond to the demands
of another day and time.

The sharp field rocks
feel right in my hands....

I gather the bold roses
emblazoned against black soil
(strong, sure hands put them there).

I gather the blood
of my ancestors.

It pulses in my veins,
calls me home.

BIRTHRIGHT

Heart of the Matter

A cross the road from the house he had built with his own hands and which had five bullets embedded in its bedroom ceiling, was the pond, manmade and stocked with fish, but, more often, used as a swimming hole—especially after he had gone to prison when it became a public domain.

In the summers, the young boys swam in its murky core, looking with blinded eyes for the gun that he had supposedly thrown there, fantasizing the water clear and bright as glass, reflecting the gun—big, bold, and blue-black—lying on its back on the silty floor. They imagined themselves bringing it to the surface, holding it high above their heads in their wet, young arms, waving it like a flag, shouting, Look, I've found it! I've found it!

But just as often, as they dove under the water, their arrow-slim bodies splitting the surface like shattering glass, they imagined her, his wife, there, rising from Poseidon's wide eye, red hair flowing, calling to them like a Siren in a softly hypnotic voice, her eyes glittering across the watery expanse.

In their nether world between heaven and hell, they floated out of time and into her arms. She held them more tenderly than did all the young girls who walked in the sunlit summer days above on the earth's surface. They drowned in her.

When he returned a few years later, the young bodies rose out of the water like sleek seals, throwing off her charms like the droplets of water they shook from themselves.

One day late in summer, enticed by the few dollars offered, some of them were gathered at a neighbor's field to put up tobacco when he walked up, offering to help. Lined up like brown soldiers, the boys jerked the loaded sticks from the ground and handed them up to him as he stood straddle-legged, balancing all the while, on the trailer behind the slow-moving tractor. With great strength, he swung the sticks up and slapped them against each other, standing them up in the back of the trailer.

At the barn, he got off, climbed up and stood astride two tiers while the boys took turns mounting the trailer and handing the sticks up to him to hang, the others watching with crossed arms from the door of the barn.

The first thing they heard was a sharp, cracking sound as one of the tiers he was standing on began to give way. Then they saw him begin to balance himself. They noticed the small cracks in his black, scuffed-up boots, made from their getting wet and drying out too many times, as he shifted them in an attempt to take some weight off the breaking tier. His arms flailing now, off balance, he used the heavy, loaded stick that he had been in the act of hanging in a now futile attempt to regain his balance, holding it, acrobat-like, above his head. The man driving the tractor looked dazed, almost asleep. The boy standing on the trailer at the time still held the next stick, poised in the act of handing it up, his eyes widening, a look of astonishment spreading over his face like water. The others stood in the barn door, feet apart, arms folded, a row of brown statues, rooted to the ground.

The next thing they heard was a crash and a sharp cry, then a long, sustained moan, then silence as the dust settled. The broken tier hung down now in two splintered pieces, and they saw him there between them, impaled on the tobacco stick that he had been about to hang, the leaves askew, partially obscuring him. The stalks of cut tobacco had slid to the end of the wooden stick that was embedded in his chest, giving it force, weighing it down. A blob of purplish blood was seeping down the front of his overalls, some of it staining the brightly golden, curing-out leaves. His head slumped over his chest, he hung there stiffly on the stick, his upper body like that of the scarecrow in the cornfield above them, his legs rubbery, turned at grotesque angles, the shoes looking too heavy now.

In that first moment of immense silence that followed, the man on the tractor began to move, heavy and uncoordinated at first. Then he was there, the horror reflected in his face. The row of young boys stood there still, apart yet irrevocably joined, feeling the dying man's pain burning in their hearts, nailing them forever to the spot.

Sorrow Times Two

S he watches as her husband plows the field, getting it ready for planting. His back to her now, leather reins around his neck, he moves forward, gently clucking to the horse, pulling expertly on the reins, holding the plow in a straight row. It is as though he and the horse are one interconnected force, the horse's head up now as the man pulls on the reins, checking him, straining backward, the horse's head down now as the man bends forward, giving him more rein.

As this force moves, machine-like, through the field, the earth turns under the plow's powerful thrusts into ribbons of dark, shiny soil. She bends over slowly and takes off her sturdy brogans. She steps into the freshly turned earth, feeling its soft coolness under her bare feet. She picks up a handful and holds it close to her face, examining with wonder the tiny, white plants, miniatures of what they will become. Almost microscopic in size and tender to the touch, they extend delicate roots through the soil's blackness.

This year, she feels a special kinship with the earth. As it quickens, sending forth new life, so she feels the stirrings of new life inside her. The baby is due soon, and she thinks as she stands there that the garden will be planted and up before it comes. Presently, she sits down on a big rock at the edge of the field, dusts off her feet, wipes her hands on her apron, puts her shoes back on, and starts back towards the house.

It is a crisp day in March, and she inhales, with deep breaths, the day's freshness, stretching her arms outward and upward. She sucks in her breath again, sharply this time, but continues to walk after a moment,

121

bending over protectively, holding the roundness of herself under her apron, clutching it to her.

At dinnertime, lunch on the table, she muses in front of the kitchen window, leaning against the basin, as her husband leads the horse to the barn, walks to the pump where he bends over, pumps vigorously until the water gushes forth, washes his hands, rubs his face briskly, then stands up and throws back his head, shaking off droplets from his shiny, black hair. Her eyes follow him dreamily as he strides through the sunlight toward the house.

Still she stands before the sink, lost in reverie so that when he appears in the open doorway, filling it up, cutting out the light, she turns her head slowly and looks at him. The softness of her face communicates something to him, and he moves toward her, putting his arms around the fullness of her. She smells his leathery smell. Placing her hands over his, she moves them downward on her stomach. I felt the baby drop today, she says. It won't be long now. It is as though his hands, so sure on the plow, shaping the earth for planting, are also shaping the very progress of the life inside of her, molding it into a likeness of him.

A few days later, she walks down the lane and stands by the fence that separates the two farms, watching her husband as he plows the neighbor's field. Movement is becoming increasingly difficult for her. As she leans against the fence, she shades her eyes from the sun and watches as he brings the horse to rest under a big apple tree at the field's edge. She sees the neighbor's daughter approaching from the house with a bucket of water. At that moment, she moves out of her body into that of the young girl's. As she moves into the shade of the tree, she feels the heat from the horse and smells its ripe smell as it stands there, exhausted from its efforts, dripping wet, its great sides moving in and out. Nostrils flaring, it shakes its head up and down, making snorting sounds, foaming at the mouth from the bit placed there. She moves alongside the horse to the man who is leaning one arm on the prow. She stands before him, smelling his leathery smell. His nostrils flare and tremble slightly as his shoulders rise and fall with his labored breathing. His face is covered with sweat, some of it running in rivulets from his eyes to his mouth, moistening it. She moves closer and feels the heat from his body, his breath hot now on her face. She offers the water up to him. His hand burns hers as he takes the dipper from her. She feels a weakness in her knees. Suddenly there is a flash of light, and she stands as before, gripping the fence post, her heavy

122

body sagging against it. In the field, the young girl is holding up a dipperful of water to her husband, the sun glancing off its tin surface.

Later that night, she turns toward her husband in bed, her forehead resting against the taut smoothness of his back, the baby moving in its own world between them. She reaches out her hand and touches his shoulder. I'm sorry, she says softly. Wordless, he turns toward her, laying his head on her breast. She cradles him there until he sleeps again.

A week later, she calls her husband from the field and tells him it is time. The month is now April, and some of the men have begun their yearly practice of gathering in the evening at the store, talking weather and crops.

They stand outside in little groups, thumbs hooked inside the galluses of their overalls, or sit on the upturned drink-bottle crates, leaning against the building. It is still light when her husband pulls his battered pickup truck in at the store. It'll only take a minute, he says, his words tumbling out rapidly in an effort to reassure her. I've got to fill up.

As they come to rest in front of the gas tanks, she notices that the front of the store is deserted. The wooden crates sit in their upright positions, empty. Her husband honks his horn, and the storekeeper comes out. His face is solemn. Something is wrong. Has someone died, she wonders distractedly. He turns the crank, jerks the hose out of his nozzle, and sticks it into the truck. She hears the gas gushing in and smells its thick, almost overpowering smell.

The storekeeper speaks to her husband through the rolled-down window as he feeds the gas into the truck's tank. Be glad you weren't here a little while ago, he says. That Beck boy just cut Old Man Mercer's youngest boy's throat. The ambulance and the law just left. He is speaking rapidly, in a low, controlled voice. He continues before her husband can warn him. It was over some girl they were both seeing. I saw it all. Joe Beck pulled up, and the Mercer kid got in the truck with him. It was right here, about where we are now. See that blood there? He motions with his head towards the ground.

She is going to faint. The truck is too hot and the smell of gas too overpowering.

It happened very quickly, the storekeeper continues. First, they were just sitting there talking, and, before I knew it, it was all over. Joe got out of the truck and waited in the store. Everybody else cleared out. I pulled his truck back there. He points with his chin to the side of the store where the truck sits, almost hidden in the shadow of the building. As best as I

123

could tell, it was self-defense. That's what I told them. I think they'll go easy on him, though, his wife being pregnant and all.

She grips her husband's arm and screams. I can't stand it! Why does it always have to happen like this?!

Not understanding, her husband, who has been sitting frozen at the wheel, turns to look at her. Don't worry, he says hoarsely. We'll get you there in no time. He is white around the mouth. He starts up the truck. I'm sorry, but we've got to go, he says to the storekeeper.

The storekeeper looks stricken. I didn't know, he says, shaking his head, heaving the hose back into its nozzle.

Her husband nods. Just put that on the book, he says, and they roar out onto the highway. Nausea grips her and forces her to scream again. Her husband takes the curves very fast, his face grim and white all over now. Hold on. We'll be there before you know it, he says, sounding breathless and shaken. But she is inconsolable, sobbing violently. Alarmed, he looks at her again, still not comprehending. Then, helpless, he reaches out one arm, pulling her to him, holding her tightly, wrestling, with his free hand and the steering wheel, the narrow, mountainous road that leads to town and the clinic. She lies against his hard shoulder, not feeling the violent jolts and twists. The pain in her heart is much greater.

Later, in the colorless hospital room, as she counts the tiny fingers and toes of her newborn baby son, she marvels at time and its power. As her husband looks at her, he wonders about the look of abject sorrow that passes over her face in that moment.

Six weeks later, after getting the baby to sleep, she moves through the darkness to her husband's side of the bed. She stands before him a moment, turns back the covers, and gets in beside him. Her slimness now matching his, she rests her body against the smoothness of his back. Instinctively, he turns towards her, awakening. She moves her body, accommodating him. His lips touch the fullness of her breasts. She moans softly. Outside, the rain begins to fall. The budding earth drinks thirstily.

124

Birthright

The scar remained, of course, even though the child died. (Years later, when she came to her husband, naked, slender as a young girl, she bore the scar of womanhood like one of a chosen people. It was pink like a baby's lips and, when he ran his finger over it lightly, smooth to the touch as a narrow, satin ribbon, though she had no feeling there.)

When it was all over, she heard someone calling her name softly, then more insistently.

Can you hear me? It's all over. You're fine now.

She tried to respond to the voices. Her throat was dry. They gave her water.

But I can't seem to open my eyes, she said.

Oh, I'm sorry. We forgot to tell you. They put some kind of jelly on them before the operation. You're all right.

She laboriously tried to stay awake. But the heavy lids, which she had finally forced open, seemed weighted, unwilling to do her bidding. She remembered her husband's face hovering closely above, taking her damp, hot hands in his, looking miserable and somehow guilty.

It's going to be all right, he said, patting her hands.

Yes, I know, she reassured him, feeling numb. But when he was gone, the waves of pain hit. Mercilessly, they rolled over her, pulling her down into darkness, almost drowning her.

The nurses hovered solicitously as she tossed.

If you want something for pain, just push the button. Almost everyone does, so don't hesitate.

125

She shook her head. She was already fighting through a fog. She didn't need anything else to hold her back.

She kept going under and coming up, her eyes still stubbornly refusing to focus.

Some time later, her husband returned, bearing gifts—flowers, candy, and fruit. (At the end of the week, the lusciously ripened pear had shriveled and blackened in the bowl.) She felt too bare before him, like a layer of skin had been removed, leaving her too vulnerable and fragile. She shrank from his touch, instinctively, perhaps imperceptibly. His touch hurt her now, his fingers heavy as her eyes. They only looked at each other—she could think of nothing to say. Tears welled up, blurring him again.

When he had gone, quietly and not reluctantly, she finally came awake. The pain was there—a dull, steady throb—but the waves that had pressed on her, pushing her to darkness again and again, threatening to force her to scream out, had subsided. The storm was over, but the wreckage was there. She felt violated, invaded. The nurses, who had been so solicitous during the day, were no longer around. They seemed to have vanished with the daylight, quickly and without warning. She lay, savoring the darkness.

At midnight, still not sleepy (since she had been in and out of sleepiness all day), she turned on the radio. Some mellow disc jockey was playing all the songs she loved—the ones where the words beat out the melody—tender words of bittersweet love and lost youth. Even though she had listened to them many times, she heard them anew, marveling at the truth of them. At six, when a new deejay came on—the other one, ever-hopeful, having signed off with Nat King Cole's "Spring Is Here"—she turned off his hip chatter—his was the road show with the work people (she heard their sounds as they struggled to the bathroom; she smelled their coffee brewing, heard their easy steps into their cars as they began their reluctant odyssey on the freeway).

Later, when the nurse came in, her arm filled with flowers, she seemed surprised.

You awake already? she said. I thought you'd sleep all morning.

Yes, I rise early, she replied. The word "rise" was her private joke, and she turned her head away, smiling to herself. It was small comfort. As the nurse waited, she pushed herself up and inched backward toward the straightbacked wooden chair by the bed. She could not straighten up, so binding was the bandage.

The breakfast arrived as she was sitting in the chair, desperately hoping that the waves of nausea wouldn't force her to ask to lie back down before the nurse had finished the practiced motions of tucking in the corners of the thin, not-quite-so-white sheets. It was clear that she was now on her own.

In order to get your strength back and go home in a week, you must try to eat everything, the nurse said, as though repeating a very familiar directive to a wayward child.

She looked at the tray. It held a mammoth meal: orange juice, milk, cooked cereal, scrambled eggs, running on the plate, a bowl of applesauce. The word "bland" was checked on the little card on the tray that bore her name. The juice was too cold and too sweet. She had never been able to eat cooked cereals of any kind, and she liked her scrambled eggs firm. But she dutifully forced the food down, seeking favor, eating mechanically like a well-trained child, pushing it in until it threatened to come up again.

Drained, drenched in sweat, she inched gratefully back onto the bed, made aware again that she was not expected to ask for assistance—the nurse had already gathered up the limp sheets and was on her way out the door.

The doctor came in later, impersonally cheerful and formal, sitting on another stiff-backed chair on the other side of the room, talking over the distance as though he were afraid of a disease or of contamination.

The next few days were routine and long. The small hospital bed, in all of its positions, became increasingly uncomfortable. She listened to her deejay at night and stared out the window during the day. (She forced herself to look into the bathroom mirror. Her gait was sluggish: she was bent like an old woman. Her hair was now dirty, greasy, looking two shades darker; her eyes, sunken into pink bruises. Her appearance contrasted cruelly with the elegance of the blue satin robe.)

It began to rain toward the end of the week, soft spring rains that forced the greenness out of the trees outside her window.

When she left on Sunday, the air was saturated with dampness, a somewhat shocking contrast to the dry, stale air inside the hospital.

Putting on clothes again for the first time was a strange experience. Nothing except her robe had touched her protesting skin. (The doctor had had the bandage removed on Tuesday. She had gasped as she sat in the chair while the nurse jerked away the wide pieces of surgical tape, looking down at the now-exposed slickly slit skin opened and zippered shut again with black stitching tied at the top. She had been frightened the first day or two as she took her obligatory walk up and down the corridor, supported by her husband, feeling embalmed and emptied as a hull, that the embroidered skin would break open and the rest of her would spill out. On Friday, the nurse had asked her to lie down as she snipped nonchalantly at the sutures with her scissors, bits of coarse, black thread flying. Your doctor does the neatest work. Your scarring should be minimal, she said.)

Her clothes hung on her as she stood shapeless before the mirror, weighing her down—too heavy, threatening to cave her in, to shatter her tender shell like glass.

A fresh-faced volunteer, her body already tanned and firm as a baby's, wheeled her into the elevator, down to the checking-out area in the lobby. Her husband trailed behind them.

Outside, for the first time in a week, she chilled momentarily in the warm, moist air, a faint breeze touching her raw skin.

At home, in her own bed, where she had often despaired of ever being again, she lay down in a fresh cotton gown under her grandmother's quilt. She asked her husband to open all the windows.

Day by day, from her bed, she watched as the gray buds of the dogwood pushed their puckered mouths open, then gradually blurred to whiteness, finally filling up the windows with spring.

Honeysuckle Rose

The house, two-storied, white weatherboarded, almost alabaster in the morning sun, stood out curiously among the brick, ranch-type houses with their neat boxwoods dotted along the main road, its lightning rods shining. Hawthorn sprawled (among iris and jonquil) in the front yard, and, in the back yard, the pink granny rose, passed down from family to family, grew tentatively among crawling honeysuckle vines that wrapped possessively around the sides of the house and, in the spring, wafted sweet scents in through the raised bedroom windows.

She lived alone there in the family house, having chosen (or been chosen) to care for her mother and father until their deaths.

He had been a classmate of hers since the first grade, but they had been friends from that day at recess when they were playing "Red Rover" and he had caught the fear in her eyes just as he burst through her clenched hand. In the next game, he had made sure that they were chosen on the same side, and he had held her hand tightly, noticing on her slim, almost skinny, white arm the red welts that he had made when he had broken through the line.

He had had, since school, several jobs, mostly odd and temporary. She had finished college and taught for three years or so at the consolidated school about ten miles away. She had given it up when she went to care for her parents and had gradually begun to farm. Each year, with the help of a tractor and temporary work hands, she raised a big garden and a crop of tobacco. She found that her still-skinny arms were surprisingly strong, and she developed an endurance and stamina that kept the help off balance and puffing. Yet, she never tanned, and a few freckles were the only evidence of her ever being in the sun. Like the old house, she, too, stood out curiously.

House and rooms have a certain atmosphere or smell all their own. He liked her bedroom in the summer, especially in the morning when the sweet scents of honeysuckle and rose, warmed by the sun, blended into a heavy, almost hypnotic smell. Sometimes he lay for two or three hours beneath her grandmother's wedding ring quilt.

When he was around thirty, the sweet smell was all too frequently joined by another smell—that of alcohol. He would sit down at the old upright piano and play "Listen to the Mockingbird." (They say that he was once offered a job at the Grand Ole Opry, but that he had turned it down, saying that he was only passing through, as usual.) She would come to sit beside him with her slim, white arms crossed, and he would see again that same fear that he had seen so many years ago. But some time later, after he had had coffee and they stood in the dark with their arms around each other and she felt his heart beat softly against hers, the fear would dissolve.

The next morning she would often slip in and gaze at him lying there, his curly hair over one eye, his face turned towards her, his left hand curved around his head and his right arm outstretched like a little child's. He liked to awaken slowly on these mornings (usually Sundays) to the sound of her voice reading. Sometimes she read until the sunlight completely flooded the room and forced them into the coolness of the kitchen where he would begin his ritual of cooking. He loved making biscuits and would duck his head obligingly while she slipped the apron around his neck and tied it around his waist. He would sing while he kneaded the dough:

"Stay all night, stay a little longer;
Dance all night, dance a little longer;
Pull off your coat, throw it in the corner;
Don't see why you don't stay a little longer."*

While the biscuits baked, they would dance soundlessly around the kitchen, dipping and bowing and smiling at each other, the familiar melody still in their heads.

The big, old house with its high ceilings was always cool when the sun didn't shine in, and she liked a fire in the fireplace in the living room, even in the summertime, After eating, he would build a roaring fire, and they would sit on the floor around the big, rock hearth until they were drowsy.

They often stretched out on the shiny, hardwood floor, their heads propped on their hands, looking at the fire over their toes. When the fire died down and the room was cool again, they would walk outside in the warm, dusky sunset and press bubbies from the sweet shrub in their hands until the little buds were warm and spicy smelling.

When he died, five years later, she gathered for his coffin masses of honeysuckle from the back yard and laced the flowing sprigs through the bouquet of pink roses picked from the family heirloom out back. She insisted that he be brought back home and invited a few family friends and the men who helped with the farm to come and sit through the night. They ate biscuits and honey, drank coffee, played the old upright, sang Bob Wills' western swing and country music, and danced until the sun rose on the alabaster house. It stood out resplendent and shining in the sun.

* *"Stay All Night (Stay a Little Longer)"*—Bob Wills, Tommy Duncan. Peer International.

Fountain of Youth

It wasn't something she had been thinking about for a long time (she told herself later), but when he appeared on the doorstep all wet with sweat and asking for help, the opportunity just presented itself, and she suddenly had to take it. (His eyes were wide and his smile so sweet.)

She usually kept her doors shut and locked, but she had just come in with the battered aluminum pitcher that she always used for watering her plants in the front yard. The evening sun came in on them, wilting them, thus they needed a lot of water in the morning. She had filled up the pitcher for a second time and started out again when she heard his step on the porch.

Before she could get to the door, he was peering in, one hand shielding those eyes from the glare so that he could see through the screen into the house. He called out, "Anyone home?" and rapped on the side of the screen door with his other hand. She walked to the door, looking at him. He started to grin and explain. "My radiator's about to blow on me. Could I get some water?" She looked over his shoulder beyond him to the road to see a dusty, red '65 Mustang convertible foaming at the mouth.

She opened the door and handed him the pitcher of water. He threw back his head and laughed. "Talk about ESP," he said. He shook his head, still amused, as he stepped off the porch, through the grass, to the car, poured in the water, slammed down the top, returned with the empty pitcher, handed it back to her, thanking her.

She nodded and took it. Still, she stood on the porch. He sat down on the steps and began to wipe the sweat from his face with the backs of his hands, wiping them off on his shirt and pants. She looked down at him. He looked up at her and then at the plants.

"Pretty," he said.

"Yes," she said.

"Would *you* like some water?" she said.

"Yes, I suppose I'd better have some, too," he laughed, "before the smoke starts coming out of my ears."

He followed her into the house and into the kitchen where she got a glass from the cabinet and started to pour him the water. She hesitated.

"Would you rather have some lemonade? I have some made," she said.

"Sounds good," he said and slid down into the chair at the head of the table, the one she always used.

She took a tray of ice and the pitcher of lemonade from the refrigerator and fixed two glasses, handing him one before sitting down opposite him with the other.

"Have some cookies," she said, taking the lid off the white ceramic jar shaped like a curled-up cat and proffering it to him. He reached in and took two of the oatmeal cookies. He had a few spots of grease on the knuckles of his well-shaped hands.

The ice tinkled companionably for the next few minutes as they drank.

"Off for the summer?" he asked.

"Yes," she answered, wondering how he knew.

"Oh, I saw the stack of letters," he said, reading her mind, pointing to the small desk near the table under the window.

She smiled. She had been catching up on some late correspondence, using the school's letterhead.

"Just passing through?" she countered, knowing intuitively just what to ask.

He nodded, smiling. "I'm at the community playhouse for the summer, painting sets."

A long pause. She smiled at him again over the ceramic cat. His eyes were bluer because of the tan; his short, curly hair bleached by the sun. He returned her smile. He had a little space between his two front teeth.

He finished his lemonade with a flourish, tanned arms flashing. "Just what I needed, and the cookies were great." He took his glass to the sink and poured out the ice. His tee shirt had pulled out a little from the back of his jeans when he bent over the car. There was a little circle of dampness in the small of his back. He walked back to the table. "One good turn calls

134

for another," he said. "Want to go for a ride? That is, if you're not chicken —knowing the history of my car."

They got into the red Mustang. It smelled of cherry lifesavers—an opened pack lay on the dashboard, melting in the sun.

"Come for a ride up the mountain?" he asked.

She nodded. He took off. She leaned back, closing her eyes, going back, feeling carefree and comfortable and young, the wind blowing her hair in her face.

Soon they were leaving the city, heading up the mountain. Her eyes still closed, she felt the temperature begin to change as they climbed higher. He was enjoying the drive, changing gears, maneuvering expertly in and out of the curves, proud of the Mustang, performing now.

With the speed and the sun and the wind and his expert driving, the ride was a sensuous one for her—all motion and undulating light. She lost track of time and place until he suddenly stopped. They had reached the top.

She opened her eyes. It had been a long time, but the place was familiar. He had parked at an overlook. Below, the town looked so far away, yet it seemed so short a time since they had been in its center.

She looked over at him and he nodded, fully appreciating her thoughts.

"How'd you like the ride?" he grinned.

"And the winner of the hill climb," she intoned in her best Howard Cosell voice, "is the daring young man in the red Mustang!" She laughed, leaning over closer to him, kissing him on the cheek. "A kiss for the winner," she said.

They got out and she took him by the hand.

"Come on. I want to show you something," she said, leading him across the road into a grassy meadow. The layers of the Blue Ridge blended into a wall of purples, surrounding them. The mountain pinks were blooming as she knew they would be, some of them already fading into hues to match the mountains.

"Impressive, isn't it?" she asked.

"Yes," he said.

She heard running water and remembered the waterfall. "Let's go wading," she said.

They took off their shoes and ran towards the water. Although expecting the coldness, she sucked in her breath sharply. "Into the fountain of youth!" she shouted. They jumped up and down in the water like children, going round and round in a circle. Then she pulled him to the mouth of the waterfall where it was deepest, the water reaching to their armpits. She pushed him down, attempting to dunk him. Into the game now, he grabbed her around the waist, pulling her down. They struggled, eyeball to eyeball, neither one giving in.

"Say 'uncle'!" she demanded

"No way!" he sputtered.

"Then kiss me!" she commanded, impulsively.

He kissed her wet lips, releasing her.

"What a way to win," he said finally, teasingly, chiding her, laughter in his eyes, still close to her.

She led him out of the water. They stretched out on the grass in their wet clothes, throwing their arms above their heads, basking in the sun. They slept the evening away, transformed into tousle-headed children.

She awoke first and watched him as he slept, as a mother watches a child. He was so relaxed that his breathing was barely perceptible. Sitting up, she took hold of one of his hands, feeling its warmth, its strength.

As the sun slipped further away, he stirred, his sleepy eyes opening. He sat up, his cheeks flushed with sleep.

"Ready to go?" he asked.

Twilight was approaching as they walked back to the red Mustang. Some lights were coming on in the town below. A family of summer tourists had just pulled up beside them and were getting out of their car, loaded with camping equipment, ready to hike to the campsites above. As they started off, the daughter in pink shorts, halter top, straw-colored hair and California tan looked back at the little red convertible and its driver and smiled appreciatively.

His eyes followed the pink shorts for a moment as he settled in. Then he looked over at her on the other side of the car.

"Like a lifesaver?" he said. "I'm afraid it's all I've got."

She laughed. "You *are* a lifesaver," she said, even as the Mustang, not failing them now, tore off down the mountain to the waiting town below.

BODY x TWO

The Dancers

Awakened by her breath
against his chest, he touches
the cool, perfect roundness
of one shoulder which shone
last night like a smooth, white stone
and traces with his forefinger
the bone that leads to the soft, sunken place
at the base of her throat,
feels the warmth of her breast,
then lets his hand rest.

Presentation

He unwraps her
as if she
were a gift

and examines her
as he would
all objects of awe

all white
all waves
all light

glistening curves
undulating
pink-tipped as a pearl

He bends his ear
to her
listening

shuddering
at her newness
her touch

all woman
all wonder
all world

Body x Two

Body x two
and I am you

sinew and bone
I atone

paint-enhanced
subdued

imbued with lewd
intellect eschewed

my womb
entombs

while your balls
balance you

Prelude to an Argument

Taste a tart retort
a crisp reply
a spicy tirade
a salty slogan
a wry riposte

Try a dash of devilry
a dollop of droll
a handful of innuendo

Pop a proverb
like a pickle
or an olive
Sop up gossip like gravy

Eat an earthy expletive
raw as escargot

Savor the mellow flavor
of a well-turned phrase
braised in irony

a heavy invective
baked, glazed in hate
calorie-laden

a healthy heaping
helping of sarcasm
steeped in sweetness
stewed in its own juices
succulent and seductive
melting like butter
in your mouth

Suck a meaty, pungent pun
stuffed with double entendre—
well-done!

Wrap a backhanded compliment
smooth and cool
bland as ice cream
around your tongue

Drool over deft funnies
crunchy and light
dipped in mischief
French-fried in malice
dusted in spite

And when you're through
sip a cup of cordiality
and try as you might
to cleanse your palate

146

Birthright

Sweet scar
of motherhood
delicate ribbon

you slice
my two selves
in half

I, a child
too young
too brave

I, a women
giving up
my life

accepting my fate
with grace
branded

my body
my birthright
brandished

Premature Births

Like old feelings
  that rise after love,
the moon, soft and white,
stirs the earth for the last time.

I move in your curve.

The night,
emptied of its dark burden,
fills with light.

The day is too soon born.

As the clouds write
their clever, indecipherable messages,
my desire becomes a kite's wish,

and the sun,
a red scar
on the unblemished day.

Son of Somnus

The moon cuts in
like an insult,
its watery rays leading to your face.

You lie in the light,
insubstantial as a dream,
moved by the moon.

Awakened, shaken by the view,
I lie by your side
watching you.

I feel you slipping away....

As the night's cover
strains over the breaking day,
I rise to push it away.

I yearn to see you
bearded and imperfect,
not journeying with the night's metaphysical miles.

You stir. I turn,
still cold and alone,
to receive your sleepy smile.

EPILOGUE

Expectations

The sky is swollen with clouds, threatening new snow. It is the day after Christmas. She stands in front of the kitchen sink scraping eggs off the plates, an air of expectancy about her. Yesterday's meal, or most of it, lies in the frostiness of the refrigerator under tinfoil. The family, not wanting leftovers tonight, have insisted on scrambled eggs.

As she scrapes the dishes, she hears the soft drone of the television in the other room, seeing in her head her husband sprawled on the sofa in front of it, half-asleep. She hears, also, somewhere there in her head, the sighs and little noises emitted by her two children who are now upstairs in their beds sleeping.

As she stands there, she sees, too, the Christmas tree in the other room with her husband, its lights still shining, crazing the icicles as they move gently in the heated air. Only *she* has insisted on leaving it up until New Year's. She can hear somewhere in her head the sounds of everyone else taking down trees, placing ornaments inside crushed tissue paper in old, yellowed boxes, taped and taped again with cellophane. She hears their collective sighs of relief as they pack everything neatly away in closets, closing the doors behind them again for another year.

As she opens the squeaky dishwasher and begins loading the plates inside, she thinks back to yesterday. As usual, it had been a time for trying too hard, smiling too much, attempting to appear interested in everyone else's lives. She hears it all in her head—empty and bright as the baubles on the tree, ephemeral as the sparkles on the then-fresh snow.

155

Now the snow is dry and gray, stacked up outside like misshapen statues where her son has cleared it away from the drive. That inevitable yet inexplicable sadness accompanying holidays, perhaps born out of high expectations and false hope, bears down on her.

As she stands there and locks the loaded dishwasher closed, she feels a stirring behind her. She turns around and he is there: the sweet, young face of her first love floats in front of her, the eyes soft and questioning. He touches a forefinger to her cheek. She knows that if she could look into a mirror she would see the print of his finger burning there. Then he drops his hand and gently takes hold of one of her shoulders. In her head, she feels her soft sweater melting under his touch, his fingers sinking into her flesh, imprinting upon her, burning into the very marrow of her bones.

Feeling the vulnerability of her body, she moves slowly towards him and, it seems, through him, hardly moving at all, not wishing to disturb the delicate tension within her. As she moves across the floor, the ticking of her heart is so loud and incessant that, in her head, she feels that the slightest jarring will cause her body to explode and spill out all her secrets and that she will become a bauble of triviality, light, weightless and hollow as a Christmas tree ornament, splashed quickly on the floor and then swept into a trash can.

As she sits down carefully in a still pulled-out chair before the kitchen table, her legs weak and rubbery, just getting her there, she knows the truth. She is not exploding at all; she is melting like the gray, misshapen statues outside. She realizes that she has been cold for so long now and that the coldness at the core of her is beginning to thaw. She is crying now, but she hears nothing except the silence—even the muffled television in the other room cannot reach her. The tears make deep ruts in her face, burning like streams of lava from the cold volcano inside, cutting into her like craters, the salty brine of bitterness cleansing, somehow releasing.

She stays frozen in that position for a long time, bent over the table, pressing her face into her apron with both hands. When she raises up, wiping her eyes with the backs of her hands like a child, feeling warm at last and relaxed as a rag doll or her two children breathing upstairs in their beds, she feels another touch on her shoulder, but it is her husband's eyes that she sees this time. Awakened now, up from the couch, he stands sleepily over her, nudging her towards the stairwell.

She moves silently up the stairs with him. In bed, long after her husband has turned over and is sleeping loudly again beside her, she listens in her head to the snow as it begins to fall, flake on flake tinkling icily upon each other, pile upon feathery pile filling up the windows. Into the night she listens until the snow covers the windows, envelops the house, until its smooth surface, soft, white, and shiny, leaves no trace of where the house has been. She sleeps, then, like a child.

About the author

Nancy Dillingham holds a degree in Literature from the University of North Carolina at Asheville. She has taught high school English, creative writing and journalism and is currently an instructor at Asheville-Buncombe Technical Community College in the continuing education department.

A native of Dillingham, N.C., she lives in Asheville, N.C., with her cat, Snowball.